445
NAC

D1445292

The Economics of Aid

LIBRARY OF MODERN ECONOMICS

GENERAL EDITOR: PROFESSOR M. H. PESTON
Department of Economics
Queen Mary College
University of London

The Economics of Aid

by J. M. Healey

WITHDRAWN STATE UNIVERSITY COLLEGE FREDONIA, NEW YORK

Beverly Hills, California

SAGE PUBLICATIONS

Copyright © 1971 by J. M. Healey

All rights reserved. No part of this
book may be reproduced or utilized
in any form or by any means, electronic
or mechanical, including photocopying,
recording, or by any information
storage and retrieval system, without
permission in writing from the Publisher.

For information address:
SAGE PUBLICATIONS, INC.
275 South Beverly Drive
Beverly Hills, California 90212

Printed in Great Britain

ISBN 0 8039 0113 5 (c)
ISBN 0 8039 0114 3 (p)

Library of Congress Catalog Card No. 70 149377

HC
60
H 383
1971b

General editor's introduction

The plight of the underdeveloped or emerging countries is one of the most pressing problems in the world today. It is often difficult for the ordinary inhabitant of an advanced country or for the student, for that matter, to appreciate the great gap between his position and that of his counterpart elsewhere in the world. The size of the gap and whether it is widening or not will be a major issue for international discussion in the years ahead. It is very closely connected with the question of economic aid which is the subject of this book.

Curiously enough, although there is a great deal of talk about economic aid, about its value, of what sort it ought to be, whether it is wasted, and so on, there is no good elementary treatment of it available. This is especially curious when it is appreciated that the subject is amenable to elementary economic analysis. The sort of techniques which the student learns are most useful in clarifying the problem of aid. At the same time, a study of these problems indicates the value of the theoretical principles and techniques that have been acquired in other courses. Thus, such matters as technical progress, the consequences of an increase in a particular factor of production, and the balance of payments are all placed into a focus which they otherwise might not get.

Dr Healey is eminently well qualified to write a book of this kind. He is an expert on both the theoretical and applied side of this and related fields. He has direct experience of underdeveloped countries and has seen for himself the kind of problems they face. The book was written while Dr Healey was a lecturer at Queen Mary College, and does not, of course, necessarily reflect the views of the Overseas Development Administration of the Foreign and Commonwealth Office, where he is currently employed.

M.H.P.

Contents

Tables

Figures

Acknowledgments

This book lays little claim to originality and owes much to the writing of many economists in recent years. The analysis in Chapter 3 is based largely on the approach pioneered by Professor Chenery and his associates and draws particularly on R. McKinnon's exposition in the *Economic Journal*, 1964. The analysis of aid tying in Chapter 6 draws on an unpublished paper by Mr J. P. Hayes and a published report by J. Bhagwati prepared for UNCTAD.

I have benefited from discussions with colleague economists in the Ministry of Overseas Development and at Queen Mary College, London. I am particularly grateful to Maurice Peston, Michael Lipton, Alf Vanags and Nick Baigent for reading the script and making critical comments and suggestions. None of these is responsible for the errors and inadequacies remaining. The opinions expressed in the book are entirely personal and do not in any way reflect the views of my employer, the Overseas Development Administration of the Foreign and Commonwealth Office.

Introduction

Many interesting books have been written on aid but most of these have been concerned with aid as an aspect of foreign policy, giving economic aspects a secondary place. Moreover there has been a tendency for writing on these subjects to be directed towards the needs of the politicians and administrators who are faced with day-to-day judgments and decisions which constitute aid policy. For this reason the literature on aid is generally rather pragmatic in its approach.

For the undergraduate and post-graduate economist a more analytical approach to aid and aid policy is desirable. This means defining aid, examining the role of aid and its allocation and assessing the effects of particular forms of aid with the concepts and techniques of economic theory, which are familiar to the student. This short study examines some of the main aspects of foreign assistance to developing countries in terms of economic principles. The book does not pretend that foreign assistance policy is, or can be, decided on purely economic criteria, but it is based on the belief that policy issues in this field are greatly clarified if they are examined from the economist's viewpoint.

It is hoped that this book will be helpful to students and teachers of undergraduate and post-graduate courses in development economics and international economics. The level of the analysis at no point should present any difficulty for a third-year economics undergraduate.

1

Aid: motives

What is aid?

Aid is an ambiguous word and there is no common agree-
ment on its definition and hence its measurement. Different
organizations and different countries include or exclude a
variety of items. Thus, the Development Assistance Committee of O.E.C.D. records the 'flow of long-term financial
resources to less developed countries and multilateral
agencies' and this includes both official flows and private
investment, private lending and export credits. Some bodies
do not record private capital flows. But it is not merely a
question of whether aid should include flows of private
resources, for official flows are very heterogeneous in
character; including outright grants, loans on different
terms of interest and repayment, funds in convertible
currency and funds which are tied to spending in one
country and which may also be tied to specific uses. Simple
aggregation is therefore almost meaningless and certainly
misleading.

One suggestion for reducing these heterogeneous cate-
gories to a common measure is to define aid as the real cost
or sacrifice to the countries providing the nominal flows of
resources. This would give aid an economic meaning. The
real cost or 'grant element' in a loan would be measured by

the difference between its nominal value and the future interest payments and amortization discounted at a rate which reflects the return on the funds alternatively open to the country supplying them. In the case of a grant the cost would obviously be identical with its nominal value.

This approach to aid measurement in terms of the economic sacrifice made by aiding countries is discussed more fully in the next chapter. A satisfactory concept of aid is particularly important for assessing the magnitude of each developed country's true aid effort and the problem of sharing the burden of assistance equitably between countries. In the rest of this chapter, however, the term 'aid' or 'assistance' will be used in the loose sense and will normally refer to the *flow of long-term official financial resources between developed and developing countries*. This includes 'bilateral' or direct government to government finance and 'multilateral' flows which are channelled through the United Nations' specialized agencies and regional bodies like the Inter-American Development Bank.

Although a measure of the cost of aid is essential for any form of burden sharing among the aiding countries, philanthropy is not necessarily required to assist growth in the developing countries. Capital flows on terms which involve no gift element at all can nevertheless benefit the recipient economy, and Chapter 3 is devoted to the process by which a *net* capital inflow can influence the growth of domestic product.

Motives

Official net flows of financial resources have been transferred from rich to poor countries on a large and growing scale in the last fifteen years (see Table 1). This is very much a post-war phenomenon and it raises the question of why it has occurred. What interests, considerations, motives have generated such a large official flow of funds and their particular geographical distribution?

Governments usually state that they provide assistance to other countries to assist their economic development. (The meaning of 'development' is examined below.) An interest in development *per se*, of course, implies a purely humanitarian motive but governments are also motivated by national self-interest. What are the self-interest motives of governments likely to be in the provision of official aid?

The following pages review some of the direct commercial political and strategic interests in aid-giving and the self-interests of the aid-givers served indirectly by assisting economic development. Statistical evidence is then considered to see what light it throws on the factors that seem to influence official assistance policies.

Commercial motives Capital flows in the form of loans at rates of interest which exceed the rate of return on investment in the lending country clearly benefit the lender commercially, but capital flows of this kind do not constitute 'aid' in the real sense. Where capital flows have some concessionary element in them, they may nevertheless, in principle, commercially benefit lenders as a whole and in the long run. This would be so if the development, resulting from aid, increased the scope for specialization and international trade. The significance of this effect is likely to be small given the size of already existing international markets for goods and given the alternative policy of reducing barriers to trade such as tariffs and quotas.

It is unlikely that these broad commercial considerations have influenced assistance policy. On the other hand there is no doubt that individual countries have provided loans on concessionary terms as a weapon to gain a competitive advantage for their *own* exports in international markets. Although national export promotion seems to be a motive, in practice it only constitutes a genuine national advantage if export earnings are worth more than their nominal value and this would imply the existence of a disequilibrium official exchange rate.

Political and strategic motives Some attempt is usually made to separate military assistance from total recorded official assistance figures, since the motive for this expenditure is clear. (Nevertheless military aid can in part be developmental in effect if the recipient would have expended some of his own resources on defence anyway.)

The offer of finance to 'keep friends and influence people' is a long-standing international practice and the desire to preserve friendly links and historical ties by offers of assistance partly accounts for (say) the concentration of U.K. assistance on Commonwealth countries. Aid becomes merely an instrument of foreign policy when its intent is to buy support for the policies of the 'assisting' country in (say) U.N. and other international forums. Aid which is effectively used to 'buy a base' for the air or naval operations of the aiding country is basically a payment for a service.

However, the political and strategic intentions of aiding governments are neither as simple nor as limited as this. If friendship or support could be merely a financial purchase, why do they usually show concern that the finance provided be used for development in the recipient country? Since there is unlikely to be significant humanitarian concern for development, the aiding governments must assume that 'aid for development' will subserve their political and strategic interests more effectively than straight subsidies or bribes.

There are several ways of questionable plausibility by which the objective of development *may* be considered to serve the self-interest of the aid-givers.

   a The régimes receiving the assistance and whose friendship or support is sought are more likely to survive if their economy is developing.

b The provision of aid for development may appear more respectable than straight subsidies and hence may gain more goodwill.

c The political stability of an area may be considered to vary directly with its level or pace of development.

What light do aid statistics throw on the relevance or importance of these different motives? Statistical evidence of two kinds is available: trends in the volume of assistance and cross-section data on the geographical distribution of aid at a particular time. These will be examined in turn.

Statistical trends

Table 1 shows the trend of total assistance between 1956 and 1967. The figures cover net *official* flows of financial resources from D.A.C. countries[1] to less developed countries and multilateral agencies (i.e. gross disbursements minus return amortization payments). Financial flows from the major individual D.A.C. countries are shown as well as *private* net investment, lending and export credits. The figures for the Communist countries are estimates and are gross figures.

During the 1950s the U.S.A. was the major contributor to total assistance but in the early 1960s a large jump in assistance levels is observable. A new plateau was reached in the 1960s with no significant upward trend and total assistance of the D.A.C. countries tended to fall as a proportion of their aggregate G.N.P.

The sharp rise in U.S. and aggregate assistance about 1960 seems to reflect various influences.

The U.S. Government publicly stated its strategic objective to be assistance for neutral and uncommitted countries to prevent them becoming dependent on Soviet aid. Although Table 1 shows no sharp rise in Communist aid disbursements at this time, their aid commitments were stepped up. Federal Germany also had cold war motives

5

for embarking on larger assistance programmes in the 1960s as it sought sympathy for its position on Berlin and East Germany among uncommitted countries.

Table 1   Official and private flow of financial resources from D.A.C. and Communist Bloc countries to less developed countries and multilateral institutions ($m)

								D.A.C. countries*		Communist bloc
			Official net flow ($m)				Private net flow	Total Private and official	Gross† disbursements
	U.S.	U.K.	Germany	Japan	Total official	% of G.N.P.			
1956	2,006	205	142	70	3,288		2,878	6,166	107
57	2,091	234	275	71	3,832		3,697	7,529	81
58	2,410	276	268	262	4,411		2,825	7,236	205
59	2,322	377	332	92	4,398		2,649	7,047	161
60	2,776	407	351	109	4,919	(0·54)	3,007	7,926	178
61	3,447	457	618	107	6,011	(0·63)	3,076	9,087	275
62	3,536	421	469	89	5,961	(0·57)	2,431	8,392	390
63	3,699	415	437	140	6,081	(0·54)	2,382	8,462	575
64	3,445	493	423	116	5,856	(0·48)	3,287	9,143	500 (?)
65	3,627	481	471	244	6,200	(0·47)	4,293	10,493	
66	3,660	526	486	285	6,498	(0·46)	3,973	10,471	
67	3,723	498	547	391	6,977	(0·46)	4,329	11,306	

* D.A.C. countries are listed in a footnote in the text. The major source of financial flow statistics on these countries is the annual O.E.C.D. *Development Assistance Review*. These figures are taken from the 1967 and 1968 Reviews. The O.E.C.D. and U.N. both publish detailed figures of long-term capital aid to poor countries.
† The figures for the Communist Bloc are estimates of economic grants and credits to non-Communist less developed countries. They are gross figures unlike the net figures for D.A.C. countries. These estimates are largely derived from calculations by the Bureau of Intelligence and Research of the U.S. Department of State. (See H. J. Arnold, *Aid for Development*, 1966, p. 162.)

A further major reason for the leap in assistance in the early 1960s was the emergence of many countries from colonial status who, admitted to the United Nations, pressed for more multilateral aid and, on independence, gained increased bilateral financial support from their former colonial rulers.

Commercial motives also played their part. West Germany, Italy and Japan had made their economic recoveries by the late 1950s and to some extent began using loan finance as a weapon to compete in export markets.

Total D.A.C. official flows have continued to rise somewhat in real as well as money terms but it is noticeable that U.S. assistance has not risen between 1963 and 1967. There is little doubt that this reflects a weakening of some of the dominant motives behind U.S. assistance programmes. Assistance has not always purchased friendship or goodwill. Assistance has not always ensured political stability and it has generally failed to achieve 'quick' results economically.

Geographical distribution

The geographical distribution of assistance rather than time trends is more likely to yield some indication of the motives or interests behind it. Thus, it is possible to statistically correlate assistance *per capita* to different countries with various country characteristics, some of which may form approximate measures of the various economic and political interests of those countries providing the assistance. For example, interest in the economic development of aided countries may be represented *prima facie* by their *per capita* income since their degree of poverty may be viewed as inversely related to their need for development and the adequacy of their domestic resources for development. There is, however, some ambiguity in this approach because low income levels may indicate a low capacity for using foreign capital effectively and hence the inadvisability of supplying large capital flows.

Table 2 shows net official financial assistance received and gross national product for different developing countries (1964–6) on a *per capita* basis. Table 3 shows the class distribution. The data in both cases refer to bilateral and multilateral assistance from D.A.C. countries. Both these tables suggest, and systematic statistical analysis confirms, that there is no significant correlation between *per capita*

7

Table 2 Per capita *G.N.P. and receipts of net official assistance by selected developing countries* from O.E.C.D./D.A.C. countries and multilateral agencies, 1964–66 annual average*

U.S. $

Recipient area/ countries	G.N.P.	Bi-lateral	Multi-lateral	Total	Recipient area/ countries	G.N.P.	Bi-lateral	Multi-lateral	Total
					America (cont'd.):				
Europe:		3·8	0·8	4·7	Argentina	650	−1·7	0·8	−0·9
of which:					Bolivia	140	8·2	1·4	9·6
Greece	510	3·6	1·6	5·3	Brazil	220	2·9	*	3·0
Spain	530	0·9	0·4	1·4	Chile	450	12·9	2·8	15·7
Turkey	240	5·4	0·4	5·7	Colombia	270	2·5	2·3	4·8
Yugoslavia	390	5·0	1·5	6·5	Ecuador	190	3·6	0·7	4·3
					Guyana	260	10·5	§	10·5
					Paraguay	200	2·8	2·1	5·0
Africa:		5·4	0·7	6·1	Peru	270	3·4	1·7	5·1
of which:					Uruguay	540	1·1	0·6	1·7
Algeria	230	14·0	0·2	14·3	Venezuela	780	0·1	3·6	3·7
Libya	210	5·3	−0·6	4·7					
Morocco	170	7·1	0·6	7·7	*Asia:*		2·8	0·3	3·2
Tunisia	180	16·7	1·2	17·9	of which:				
U.A.R.					Iran	210	0·4	0·3	0·7
(Egypt)	150	4·6	0·1	4·7	Iraq	240	1·0	0·2	1·2
Burundi	50	1·7	0·5	2·3	Israel	1,070	41·8	8·5	50·3
Congo					Jordan	220	25·9	10·7	36·6
(Kinshasa)	140	7·1	0·6	7·7	Kuwait	3,290	†	−4·0	−3·9
Ethiopia	50	0·9	0·4	1·2	Lebanon	390	0·4	3·4	3·8
Ghana	230	6·0	1·6	7·6	Saudi				
Guinea	70	3·7	1·1	4·9	Arabia	190	*	−1·1	−1·1
Kenya	90	6·4	0·4	6·8	Syria	180	−0·3	0·9	0·6
Liberia	180	30·4	1·2	31·6	Yemen	90	1·1	0·1	1·1
Malawi	40	8·3	‡	8·3	Afghanistan	85	3·2	0·2	3·3
Nigeria	100	1·5	0·5	2·0	Burma	60	0·7	*	0·7
Rwanda	50	2·4	0·6	3·0	Ceylon	130	1·6	0·2	1·8
Sierra Leone	120	5·3	0·6	5·9	India	90	2·2	0·3	2·5
Somalia	50	7·4	1·5	8·8	Nepal	70	1·6	0·1	1·7
Tanzania	70	3·3	0·3	3·6	Pakistan	90	3·7	0·5	4·2
Uganda	80	2·8	0·3	3·1	Cambodia	120	1·6	0·3	1·9
Zambia	160	6·1	−0·7	5·4	China				
African &					(Taiwan)	190	3·9	0·8	4·8
Malagasy					Hong Kong	320	0·5	*	0·6
States	§	5·6	2·2	7·8	Indonesia	70	0·6	*	0·6
					Korea				
					(South)	120	7·0	0·1	7·1
America:		3·4	1·0	4·4	Laos	60	22·8	0·3	23·1
of which:					Malaysia	260	2·2	1·3	3·5
Costa Rica	360	8·0	5·9	13·9	Philippines	140	2·2	0·4	2·7
Dominican					Thailand	110	1·4	‡	1·4
Republic	210	14·2	0·1	14·2	Vietnam				
El Salvador	260	4·4	1·3	5·7	(South)	110	22·1	‡	22·1
Guatamala	290	2·3	−0·1	2·2					
Haiti	75	0·9	0·2	1·0	*Oceania:*				
Honduras	360	3·9	1·2	5·1	of which:				
Jamaica	430	4·2	0·7	4·9	Papua &				
Mexico	430	0·6	1·2	1·8	New				
Nicaragua	320	5·1	2·9	8·0	Guinea	§	37·3	‡	37·3
Panama	450	16·9	1·7	18·6					
Trinidad &					*Total recipient*				
Tobago	590	12·5	3·3	15·9	*countries*		3·6	0·5	4·1

* Major recipients of Sino-Soviet aid commitments in recent years include India, Indonesia, Pakistan, Iran, U.A.R., Syria, Afghanistan, Brazil and Algeria.

Source: Development Assistance Review, 1968, p. 271

† = negligible ‡ = incomplete § = not available

assistance and *per capita* income level of the recipient. If a recipient's capacity for development is indicated by its recent growth rate then, once again, statistics do not reveal that the providers of assistance systematically allocated their aid in this way.

Of course, 'political' influences are least likely to show up statistically in aggregate data on foreign aid since the political

Table 3   Relationship between aid receipts per capita, *1964–6 and gross domestic product per head, 1965*

Average net official per capita *aid receipts* (*Bilateral & multilateral*)	Number of countries					
	Gross domestic product					
	Under $100	$100 *to under* $200	$200 *to under* $300	$300 *to under* $500	$500	*Total*
Under $2	4	4	4	2	4	18
$2 to under $4·1*	4	1	1	3	1	10
$4·1* to under $10	5	19	9	4	3	40
$10 to under $20			3	2	3	8
$20 to under $50		1	2			3
$50 and more					1	1
Total	13	25	19	11	12	80

* Average of all recipient countries
Source: *Development Assistance Review*, 1968, p. 147

and strategic interests and ties of different aid-giving countries are likely to offset one another. However, data in Table 2 reveal a few countries which receive extremely high levels of bilateral aid *per capita* which clearly reflects their strategic position on the fringe of the Communist Bloc or in areas of vital concern to the Western powers (e.g. Vietnam, Laos, Jordan and Israel).

A systematic relationship between the scale of aid and size of receiving country is observed for total D.A.C. aid distribution and also for individual aid-giving countries. There appears to be some minimum quantum of aid regardless of size of country, which means that small countries receive disproportionately large amounts of aid.

This result may reflect development considerations in so far as small countries require assistance for minimum irreducible administrative overheads. It may also reflect political influences – the relatively favourable treatment which has been extended by major powers (especially U.K. and France) to small colonies which have recently become independent. This 'dependency' effect reflects the obligation imposed on the assisting country by historical ties and also the desire to preserve friendly future ties with ex-colonies.

After this brief review of influences on the actual pattern of the allocation of net flows of official financial resources, it is necessary to look more carefully at the aid objective which is of most interest to the economist – aid for development.

Aid for development

Official aid is often provided ostensibly for the development of the receiving country although it has already been pointed out that this may be only one objective among many of aid-giving countries. It is now necessary to consider more carefully the meaning of development and how aid is expected to assist it.

The term 'development' covers many different types of change. From various academic viewpoints it includes notions of industrialization, urbanization, modernization, westernization or changes in value systems from those which are tradition-based to those which are achievement-orientated. From an economic perspective development can be measured (though not defined) by the market value of the quantity of goods and services available per person. Development can then be said to occur when there is an observed increase in gross national product *per capita*, i.e. when G.N.P. grows faster than population.

The inadequacies of this statistical measure of development are all too obvious. It cannot be identified with an improvement in economic welfare for an arithmetic mean does not yield even the crudest indication of the distribution of output (income) between people, groups or regions. It cannot be identified with an improvement in total welfare for it takes no account of the displacement of traditional crafts, the dislocation of kinship groups and the tensions that arise in a society where new values and aspirations (required for increased production for the market) conflict with traditional ones.[2]

However, this crucial issue of what really constitutes development and what would be an adequate index of development takes us beyond the realms of economics into sociology, psychology, anthropology, etc. The reader who wishes to pursue these much wider and deeper matters is referred to a short bibliography at the end of this book. In order not to be grounded from the start the following economic analysis will use G.N.P. *per capita* as a measure of development despite its obvious deficiencies.

With development measured this way the contribution of aid to development will depend on the growth of population and the growth of G.N.P. Population growth may be viewed as given and independent of aid and G.N.P. growth, since historically, accelerated population growth appears to have resulted largely from falling death rates which in turn have been due to exogenous influences. However, population growth is clearly not completely independent of aid flows or growth of output since aid in the form of technical assistance (e.g. medical assistance) may reduce death rates while increased output of domestic goods and services affects the health and the nutrition of the population and hence mortality rates. These relationships and their importance have not been fully examined or estimated by social scientists. For this reason attention here will be focused only on the contribution of aid to growth of G.N.P. of the recipient economy.

11

Economists often take a formal approach to the aid/ growth relationship. A model of an economy is built with a number of variables which have technological or behavioural relationships and which are often fixed coefficients. The growth of G.N.P., the key variable, is then seen as limited by certain domestic constraints in the economy. These constraints on growth may be classified into three types, all of which may be relieved by external resources.

First, there is the *savings* constraint on growth which is familiar from the Harrod-Domar type model of economic growth. Secondly, there is the constraint imposed by the domestic supply of certain *strategic goods*. This arises if all outputs require inputs in fixed coefficients as in a Leontief type of input–output model of an economy. Thirdly, there may be a constraint on growth imposed by the domestic availability of certain types of *skills*. The role of external assistance can then be seen as supplementing those domestic resources which constitute the dominant bottlenecks on growth.

This view of the different roles of aid in growth is still somewhat controversial. Not all economists agree that these are separable constraints on growth, and this aspect of economic theory is discussed more fully in Chapter 3.

It must be stressed at this stage, however, that the economists' approach, via models and bottlenecks, which is spelt out later in this book, is a somewhat mechanical one. Growth is seen essentially as something which can be programmed by feeding in the appropriate quantities of the appropriate resources. It largely ignores the qualitative factors, the underlying value systems, human responses to financial and other stimuli, institutions and the policies of the domestic government, or else it assumes that these will be favourable to growth.

Although there is little possibility that inflows of foreign assistance will have any direct and significant effect on local values, attitudes and institutions, the provision of aid may be made *conditional* on the domestic government following policies which seem likely to favour growth. Whether this potential 'leverage' effect of aid constitutes an addition to the purely 'resource' effect will depend on whether such a strategy is 'politically' acceptable to the aid-recipients and whether the aid-givers know more than the aid-recipients about the types of policy which are most appropriate in the particular conditions of the country concerned. The 'leverage' effect of aid on growth is clearly something which cannot be subjected to the formal analysis which is later applied to the role of assistance as supplementation of specific domestic resources.

Notes

1 The D.A.C. countries include Australia, Austria, Belgium, Canada, Denmark, France, Germany, Italy, Japan, Netherlands, Norway, Portugal, Sweden, Switzerland, United Kingdom, and United States.
2 Development would seem to involve a basic paradox that if people want to get more of what they value then changing their values is a prerequisite for satisfying this desire.

2

Aid: allocation principles

The description in the previous chapter does not represent, in any sense, an ideal situation. Aid has not been clearly defined in practice. The provision of development finance has been a largely nationalistic and often competitive activity and only limited movement has been made towards viewing and organizing assistance as a co-operative international activity in which the burden of aid might be shared equitably between countries and the allocation of aid might be based on clear common objectives.

This chapter will examine some of the important conceptual issues that would arise in a rather more ideal world of international co-operation for foreign assistance to less developed countries. This will cover (*a*) the definition and measurement of genuine aid; (*b*) the international sharing of the cost of assistance; (*c*) the optimum allocation of assistance among different countries.

The definition and measurement of aid

What is aid? Aid is a gift. However, only a part of the financial resources transferred from rich to poor countries is actually in the form of outright grants, while loans clearly cannot be entirely gifts if they have ultimately to be repaid with or without interest. There may be a gift element in loans and if this can be measured then grants and loans on different terms can all be reduced to one comparable standard.

From the point of view of the lender, 'aid' is the real cost of providing the loan, and the real cost of the resources lent or given is the benefit forgone by not using them in their best alternative use. In this calculation of the opportunity cost of assistance there are two major considerations.

First, the cost will depend on the terms of the loan, interest rate, grace period and repayment schedules. Second, it will depend on the conditions of the loan or grant, i.e. whether the goods which can be obtained by the recipient are valued at their opportunity cost. In other words the real cost of loans depends on the gift element in money terms but also the extent to which the value of commodities made available under these loans differs from their value if the donor disposed of them in a different way.

It is useful to begin by ignoring the second complication and take it up later.

The next three sections may prove difficult for students who have not been introduced to the concept of the discount rate and its use in investment economics. They might consult a companion volume in this series, J. L. Carr's *Investment Economics*.

The terms of assistance

The real cost of aid will depend on the terms on which the monetary flows are provided. If they are in the form of grants then the nominal value and real cost will be identical. The donor has forgone the use of these financial resources forever. If they are in the form of a loan the lender loses the use of these resources initially but their use is not completely forgone but only postponed since the loan will be repaid in future instalments and the lender may also receive interest payments. Hence the real cost is the difference between the present value to the lender of the future flow of repayments and interest and the magnitude of the initial loan.

In assessing the present value of future return flows from the borrower it is necessary to consider the lender's alternative policy of investing the loan funds at home at a positive rate of return. To put the question another way, what sum invested now in the donor country at the current rate of return would yield a flow of income equal to the repayments and interest expected from the borrower? The answer lies in discounting the future repayments and interest at the rate of return which could have been earned by the lender if, alternatively, the funds had been invested at home.

The present value of an aid loan will then depend on the rate of interest charged relative to the rate of return on investment in the donor country and the period of repayment of the aid loan. The higher the rate of return in the donor country (given the rate of interest on the loan) the greater will be the opportunity cost to the donor. Also the longer the period of repayment of the loan, other things being equal, the greater will be the cost. Thus an interest-free loan of £100 repaid in equal annual instalments over 25 years will cost the donor £30·4 if discounted at 3% but £48·9 if discounted at 6%. If it is repaid over 50 years the cost will be £48·5 and £68·5 respectively. The loan is costless to the lender if the rate of interest is identical with the lender's alternative rate of return. If the rate of interest on the loan exceeds the lender's opportunity cost the lender will, of course, benefit from aid on these conditions. Table 4 sets out the cost or grant element of loans on different terms.

When real aid flows are distinguished they emerge as considerably smaller than foreign assistance flows conventionally defined. Table 5 shows statistics for 1965. It is noticeable that the level of genuine aid was on average three-quarters of conventionally measured official assistance from D.A.C. countries in 1965. There was also considerable inter-country variation in the grant element of assistance although

Table 4   Grant element in loans with different interest rates and maturities

		\multicolumn{6}{c}{Lenders' rate of discount}					
Terms of loan		5%	6%	7%	8%	9%	10%
Rate of interest	Maturity* (yrs.)						
2%	20	22·1	27·8	32·8	37·6	41·7	45·5
	30	28·9	35·7	41·5	46·6	51·0	54·7
	40	34·2	41·5	47·5	52·5	56·9	60·5
3%	20	14·7	20·8	26·3	31·3	35·8	39·8
	30	19·3	26·8	33·2	38·8	43·7	47·8
	40	22·8	31·1	38·0	43·9	48·7	52·9
4%	20	7·4	13·9	19·8	25·0	29·8	34·1
	30	9·6	17·8	24·9	31·1	36·4	41·0
	40	11·4	20·7	28·6	35·0	40·5	45·3
5%	20		6·9	13·1	18·6	23·8	28·4
	30	0	8·9	16·6	23·3	29·2	34·2
	40		10·4	19·0	26·3	32·5	37·7
6%	20			6·6	12·5	17·9	22·7
	30	0	0	8·4	15·5	21·8	27·4
	40			9·6	17·5	24·3	30·1
7%	20				6·3	11·9	17·1
	30	0	0	0	7·8	14·5	20·5
	40				8·8	16·2	22·6

* No grace period in repayment is assumed.
Source: Adapted from G. Ohlin, *Foreign Aid Policies Reconsidered*, O.E.C.D., 1966, pp. 111–12.

the use of this measure does not significantly change the country 'ranking' in aid performance for 1965.

From the borrower's viewpoint the real value of a loan (or grant) may differ from the real cost to the lender. The

17

Table 5 Grant element and gross official disbursements to developing countries by D.A.C. countries in 1965

1965 Figures	*(1)* Grant element as % of total commitments	*(2)* As % of national income Total gross official flows	*(3)* Grant element in gross official flows	*(4)* Rank according to *(3)*
U.S.	81	0·67	0·60	4
Sweden	95	0·25	0·24	10
Canada	79	0·34	0·31	9
Denmark	78	0·17	0·16	15
Australia	100	0·64	0·64	3
France	87	1·08	0·98	1
Germany	62	0·50	0·44	7
Norway	98	0·22	0·20	12
U.K.	75	0·61	0·52	5
Belgium	99	0·90	0·83	2
Netherlands	84	0·41	0·32	8
Austria	29	0·49	0·18	14
Italy	33	0·22	0·19	13
Japan	53	0·37	0·22	11
Portugal	59	0·75	0·48	6
Total D.A.C.	77	0·61	0·55	

Countries are ranked in descending order of national income per head. In calculating the grant-element of gross official flows (disbursements) a 10% discount rate was used. It should be noted that there is often inconsistency between the ratio of $\frac{\text{column (3)}}{\text{column (2)}}$ and column (1) because column (1) refers to commitments of funds and column (2) to disbursements.

Source: Development Assistance Efforts and Policies, 1966 and 1967 Reviews.

value of a loan will depend on the rate of return on investment in the *borrowing* country and this may differ from that in the lending country. Thus, if the borrower's rate of return (or rate of discount) is greater than the lender's, the real value of a loan to the borrower will be greater than the real cost to the lender and vice versa.

If the official exchange rate of the borrowing country is a 'disequilibrium' rate, the value of the foreign exchange resources provided by the loan needs to be adjusted by an appropriate 'shadow' exchange rate. This may alter the recipient's rate of return on aid resources compared to domestic resources.

'Tying' and the value of aid

In addition to the terms of aid and discount rate, the extent to which transfers of funds are 'tied' to procurement of goods in the lending country may also affect their value to the recipient and their cost to the lender.

Loans tied to use in the lending country may reduce their value to the borrower compared to a situation in which the funds could be used to buy goods from the cheapest or most preferred international source. Although tying will normally reduce the value of loans to the recipient they will not necessarily reduce the real cost to the lender. If resources are fully employed in the lending economy the real cost of the tied loan is not reduced unless the particular industries supplying the aid goods are able to exploit a monopolistic advantage over the borrower by charging prices which exceed the opportunity cost of the goods supplied. This is possible but not inevitable and assumes collusion among firms in an industry when meeting orders on tied aid.

If aid purchases are tied to industries where resources are unemployed, on the other hand, the opportunity cost of the goods supplied may be less than the price actually charged. In the short-run, capital and skilled labour in an industry (e.g. shipbuilding) may be immobile and their opportunity cost zero, even if materials used in production have alternative uses. Tying aid to 'surplus capacity' industries of this kind clearly reduces the real cost of aid on the assumption that the government would not otherwise undertake spending to activate the idle capacity for domestic use. Aid funds tend, in practice, to be spent on 'growth' industries where there is normally little idle capacity. The countries receiving

C

aid often have their own capacity to produce the more 'traditional' products and these tend to be the 'declining' industries in the lending countries where excess capacity may well exist. Hence, except where aid is tied to specific industries, it would be somewhat coincidental if aid expenditure generally fell on industries with spare capacity.

When tying takes the form of resources provided in kind, the 'gift' element of these resources will depend on the valuation placed on the goods, even when they are provided nominally on a grant basis. Food (wheat) surpluses provided under U.S. Public Law 480[1] are an important case in point. In practice these food surpluses have been partly valued at a price originally paid to U.S. farmers under the price support programme and partly valued at current world market prices which are lower. In both cases the wheat is overvalued. An extreme view would be that the resource cost of surplus food output to the U.S. is zero because the factors producing it are immobile – they have no alternative employment. The value to the recipient of this food grant, however, would be positive depending on the international price that it would have had to pay for food. However, even the current world market price may overstate the alternative value of the wheat to the U.S. because the quantum of wheat supplied on U.S. aid has often constituted a large proportion of total world trade in wheat (often 25%). Hence, the alternative course of selling the 'aid' wheat in the world market would depress prices unless the elasticity of world import demand were infinite. More plausibly, assuming the elasticity of demand not to exceed unity, the alternative value of P.L. 480 wheat would have been at least 25% less than its value at current world prices. This would reduce the real cost of food aid to the U.S. but would not alter its value to the recipient.

To sum up, therefore, it has been shown that the nominal value of 'aid' flows normally recorded in the official statistics of donor countries, do not necessarily represent the real cost to the donor country (or the real value to the recipient).

The true aid element in so-called 'aid' programmes can be derived only when allowance has been made for the terms on which the funds are provided and adjustments made for goods supplied on 'aid' whose recorded value exceeds their opportunity cost. Efforts to share the cost of aid equitably among donors should clearly be based on this real cost concept. This issue of burden sharing will be taken up a little later.

Minimization of the cost of aid

The preceding analysis provides a measure of the cost of foreign assistance to the countries providing the assistance; it also provides criteria for minimizing the burden of assistance to the donor.

Of course, one way of minimizing the cost of foreign assistance is to provide none. However if the provider of assistance aims to achieve a *given real present value* of benefit to the recipient, then it is possible to minimize the cost of doing this by varying the terms of assistance. The following formal propositions can then be established.

1 To achieve a given present value of benefit to the recipient, grants cost the donor less than loans if the yield on capital is higher in the donor country than the recipient country and vice versa.

Although the general proof of this proposition requires mathematics the reason is apparent. Resources are being shifted from an economy which uses them more effectively to one which uses them less effectively. To achieve the same present value to the recipient, a loan must transfer more resources *sooner* than a grant because it has to be serviced. The earlier the resources are transferred the greater the cost to the provider of these resources. This can be illustrated by an example. Suppose the rate of return on investment is 7% in the recipient economy and 8% in the donor economy.

21

Let the choice lie between a £100 loan for 50 years at 6%
or a grant equal to the present discounted value to the
recipient of the flow of benefits from the loan. The grant to
provide the recipient with the same benefit would have to
be £13·8.[2] What is the cost to the donor of these alternatives?
In the case of the loan the cost is £2 per annum for 50 years
(i.e. difference between £6 annual interest received and £8
yearly alternative return if £100 were invested at home).
The present value of this annual cost, discounted at 8%, is
£24·5. The cost of the grant is £13·8 and this is clearly more
economical.

On the other hand, if the rate of return on capital is higher
in the recipient country than the donor country, a loan would
cost the donor less than a grant for the same aid benefit to the
receiver. It is worth noting that grants always cost the donor
something but a loan need not. If the yield on capital is
larger in the recipient than in the donor economy it is clearly
possible to have an interest rate which provides a net gain
to the recipient and the donor.

2   To achieve a given present value of benefit to the recipient
when the yield on capital is higher in the donor than in the
recipient economy: (a) Smaller loans at lower rates of interest
cost the donor less than larger loans at higher interest rates,
and (b) smaller loans for longer periods cost less than larger
loans for shorter periods. These formal propositions are
another application of the principle set out in 1 above.

The policy implications of these criteria seem clear but
their application in practice is somewhat qualified. First,
since the rules assume that donors and recipients assess
grants and loans by their present value it requires the
recipient to be capable of investing and disinvesting freely
at the yields on capital prevailing. Since projects financed
by foreign assistance are usually large and lumpy the yields
at any stage in the project may not reflect yields elsewhere.
Further, yields are rarely known with accuracy in different

economies even if it is assumed that they are equated at the margin in all investments. Thirdly, recipients may default on loan repayment. The existence of this uncertainty may oblige the donor, who would otherwise choose loans, to provide grants to ensure that recipients with low yields on capital receive any benefits at all (i.e. to cover the risk of default by a higher interest rate may raise the interest rate above the rate of return in the recipient country). Finally, there are also non-economic reasons for deciding the terms of assistance. For example, psychologically and politically it may be desirable to provide loans rather than grants. The notion of 'charity' can have a demoralizing effect on the recipient.

International cost sharing

The measure of aid described above provides a standard for comparison of the true contribution of different nations to the development process in poor countries. It would, therefore, form the basis for any scheme for sharing the cost or burden of assistance between countries.

So far no comprehensive scheme of this kind has been developed, although there have been some *ad hoc* moves towards greater joint effort in the provision of aid. If foreign assistance did become entirely an area of co-operative international activity there would have to be some method of cost sharing devised. This would be an exercise in international public finance, and it could not be solved purely on the basis of economic theory. However, the literature of public finance has produced two main principles for the sharing of costs of certain public services between different groups within national boundaries. These two principles – the Benefit Principle and the Ability to Pay Principle – will now be examined in the context of international assistance for development of the poorer nations.

23

a *Benefit principle*

The essence of the benefit principle is that each contributor makes a payment that is a *quid pro quo* for the benefit received. It is a principle that is unlikely to provide a guide for international aid sharing because many of the benefits to the donors will be 'collective'. Indeed, it might be argued that cost-sharing arises only when the benefits are diffused and not directly related to the individual donor's aid.

There are some benefits from aid-giving such as immediate commercial advantages (export promotion) or the 'moral glow' from providing aid from humanitarian motives, which accrue directly to the nation providing the aid and to no one else. However, some of the benefits (real or imaginary) are collectively enjoyed. In the case of the economic gains[3] of aid-giving it is possible, in principle, to distinguish the gains accruing to individual donors but virtually impossible in practice. When one of the benefits of aid is believed to be improved world 'security' it is clearly a collective benefit which cannot be allocated among the contributors.

b *Ability to pay principle*

The 'ability to pay' principle is based on the idea of equal sacrifice, but in determining criteria for sharing the cost of 'aid' several important conceptual and empirical problems arise.

a First, should ability to pay be formulated in terms of 'nations' or 'individuals' as units? On grounds of convenience nations would be chosen, but in an integrated world community it may be contended that the burden of international activities for the common welfare should be related to individual capacities to pay rather than the capacities of nations.

b Second, there is no objective basis for interpreting the 'ability to pay' principle as a proportional or progressive 'tax' system (or for determining the actual progressive rate

24

structure to be used internationally). If the 'nation' is to be the unit, then equality of sovereign states might suggest a proportional basis for burden sharing. On the other hand, most nations follow a progressive system of taxation internally, and this would suggest a similar system internationally.[4] If a progressive system is chosen, assessment of the aid contributions on the basis of *per capita* national income ignores the problem of equity between *individuals* in different nations. For this reason some economists have suggested that international taxation should be based on a 'world' distribution of income among individuals with each country paying a part of the total equal to the proportion its nationals would pay under a worldwide progressive personal tax system. This would still leave the finance to be raised by national governments and there would remain scope for inequity depending on the particular tax structure used by each government or whether the provision of aid involves *incremental* taxation which may not necessarily be progressive at the margin.

c Thirdly, there are problems in comparing the national income of different countries owing to differences in concept and coverage of national accounts statistics and the problem of using official exchange rates which do not always provide an accurate guide to the relative purchasing powers of national currencies. Similar problems would apply to data used for a 'world income distribution'.

Allocation of aid

The assumption of international co-operation to share the burden of aid-giving does not necessarily affect the distribution of aid, since individual donors could distribute their share of aid according to their own national objectives. However, let us now assume that aid *distribution* is handed over entirely to some multilateral agency. It might then be assumed, somewhat unrealistically,[5] that such a body would be 'politically disinterested' in aid-giving, unlike most national donors whose country-wise aid allocations are influenced by historical ties, ideology, national foreign policy purposes, etc.

If this were the case, on what principles would the multi-lateral agency distribute its aid resources? Can any purely objective criteria be devised?

Many criteria or aid strategies have been suggested. Three are discussed below: (a) The redistribution principle. (b) Achieving 'self-sustained' growth. (c) Maximizing the development effect of aid.

1 *Pure redistribution of incomes*

Given the inequality in *per capita* incomes between nations there is a case on ethical grounds for poor relief – an inter-national redistribution of income from rich to poor involv-ing some form of 'utility' weighting. This might take the form of a progressive tax system on the rich countries and sub-sidies to the poor countries which would vary inversely with their poverty. On this principle there would be no obliga-tion for the subsidy receivers to use the resources for develop-ment purposes and they could use them to make a net addition to their own consumption. The donors would be obliged to provide assistance entirely in grants.

There are some obvious objections to this principle in its pure form. Consumption subsidies would have no lasting effect,[6] in situations where population growth impels some development effort. Moreover, in practice, inadequate resources are likely to be redistributed to make much impact on the degree of international inequality.

2 *Achievement of self-sustained growth*

Another possible strategy is to concentrate limited aid resources on those countries which are likely to achieve 'self-sustained growth' within a given period of time. The idea of self-sustained growth is that a judgment can be made about the possibility of a country achieving and maintaining a specified growth rate eventually without external assistance. Given a growth rate considered 'satisfactory' it is possible, in principle, to predict the time required for an economy to become independent of external assistance while achieving the desired growth rate. One method of doing so is to assume that growth is largely a function of capital accumulation and to construct a model of an economy which places plausible empirical values on the main parameters like the yield on capital, the savings rates, etc. (The following chapter is devoted to this particular problem.) Since some economies would have greater growth potential than others it is possible to have a strategy of concentrating aid on all those countries likely to sustain the required growth themselves within (say) 10 years or 20 years. This is the strategy of getting 'as many horses past the finishing post as possible in a given time'.[7] The aid distribution which would result from this principle would be very different from that based on the pure redistribution principle since the 'horses' likely to finish quickest are not likely to be the poorest ones.

There would seem to be little or no ethical or political justification for such a strategy. Is there an economic justification?

Some economists have put forward the hypothesis of a 'population trap' to economic development. One crucial proposition in this hypothesis is that up to a point an increase in income *per capita* will induce (with a lag) an increase in the rate of population growth which *offsets* the increase in the rate of growth of income feasible at the higher standard of living. Aid which raises income *per capita* will only lift a country clear of this trap and allow income growth to exceed population growth if it is available in sufficiently large doses. If limited aid were concentrated on a few countries therefore, it might allow them to break out of the trap. If spread over many it might lift none out of the trap.

The hypothesis is somewhat extreme: it is doubtful if

27

population growth is such a rigid function of income standards and there needs to be a particular combination of
empirical values of the important growth variables for the
hypothesis to hold in practice in many countries.[8]

3 *Maximization of development effects of aid*

A criterion fairly close to the allocation rules of orthodox
economic theory is that scarce aid resources should be distributed between countries so that at the margin a unit of aid
has the same development impact everywhere. The 'development effect' of aid may then be formally defined as the present
value of all future increments of consumption resulting
from the aid. This calculation gives rise to two problems.
First, there is the problem of estimating the effects of various
quantities of current aid on future consumption in each
country. In principle, 'objective' estimates of this kind can
be made which will be discussed shortly. Second, there is the
problem of comparing present and future units of consumption and comparing the value of a unit of consumption in
different countries. In both cases some form of weighting
is required which will express the donor's preference between
present and future generations and between different countries. There is no 'objective' way of doing this and it is a
matter of judgment, for example, what different weights
should be given to a unit increase in present consumption
in countries with different *per capita* income levels and different cultures. This raises all the familiar problems of inter-
personal comparisons of utility and whether the utility of
marginal real consumption declines.

The marginal effectiveness of aid involves, at least, an
assessment of the direct and indirect effects of external
capital on the national income of the recipient in all future
periods. The *direct* effect is the permanent net addition to
national income – this might be called the yield or productivity of external capital. There are reasons for believing
that it may be a declining function of the scale of the capital

28

inflow in a given period of time, because of the scarcity of complementary domestic factors such as skilled manpower in the short period.[9] The *indirect* effect of foreign capital arises from the direct increment of income. The savings out of this extra income (the marginal saving rate) will be invested and in turn add further to income and so on. There is a multiplier effect over time whose size will depend on the productivity of capital and on the marginal savings rate in the country concerned.[10] Although normally the indirect effects of investment are ignored and income saved is not valued differently from income consumed, the justification for taking account of different national marginal savings rates in aid allocation is that the aid-giving agency may wish to discount the future at a different rate from the government or people of the recipient country. The donor establishes for each recipient its *own* value of aid by computing all future increases of consumption (consequent on aid) while discounting them at its *own* rate of discount. This value of aid concept is then comparable between recipients.

Notes

1 Some P.L. 480 aid is formally on a grant basis. These loans are interest free and repayment is required in the local currency. Since these repayments cannot effectively be used to buy foreign currencies or to export the recipient's products, the loans really constitute grants.

2 i.e., the annual net benefits to the recipient of the £100 loan invested at 7% are £1 per year for 50 years (i.e. £7 minus interest charge of £6). When this stream of benefits are discounted to the present and summed they equal £13·8.

3 Economic benefits are the increased trade possibilities for the donor countries in the long run following growth of the less developed countries from aid.

4 Empirically it would appear that the distribution of income (*per capita*) between nations is more unequal than the distribution between income groups within the developed countries.

5 It is unrealistic since such a body would reflect the interests of the major donors in its strategy as the World Bank has tended

to reflect U.S. ideology in practice. In any case it would develop a political bias of its own.

6 Unless it is assumed that higher levels of personal consumption increase people's productivity directly and significantly.

7 See I. M. D. Little and J. M. Clifford, *International Aid*, pp. 98–9.

8 For a critical account of this hypothesis see H. Myint, *Economics of Developing Countries*, Ch. 7.

9 The productivity of external capital is a complex concept. The net addition to national income resulting from foreign capital may exceed the yield on capital since idle natural resources or unemployed manpower may be brought into use.

10 At infinity, one unit direct addition to annual national income (from invested capital) will have grown to $\dfrac{1}{1-\delta\bar{s}}$ where δ = output/capital ratio and $\bar{s}$ = marginal saving rate.

3

Aid and economic growth I

Aid and growth

The transformation of a poor country with a low or zero growth rate into one capable of an adequate sustained growth rate is the essence of the development problem.[1] Faster growth requires an improvement in the skills of a country's labour force, a growth in its capital stock, and substantial changes in the composition of output and accompanying changes in attitudes and institutions. Although only the most mechanically-minded economist believes that there is a fixed relationship between foreign resource flows and the growth rate of the receiving country, nevertheless, it is helpful to spell out formally the ways in which foreign assistance can augment a country's capital stock, imports of specific commodities and skills and so remove *some* of the constraints on growth in a society which would otherwise have to depend entirely on its domestic resources.

This section will attempt to show that the impact of foreign assistance on the growth of a poor country will depend on what are the dominant constraints on growth – whether savings, foreign exchange availability or skills. It will go on to consider the conditions under which aid flows will permit growth to become ultimately self-sustaining.

Two roles of foreign assistance

If skill problems and other institutional requirements for growth are ignored there are two views of the contribution of foreign capital assistance to economic growth.[2]

The first view sees the maximum level of domestic savings as the dominant constraint on growth, and foreign capital as a supplement for domestic savings which permits higher investment and growth. In this view, domestic capacity is assumed to provide the required import of foreign goods, (via exports) provided domestic consumption is restrained enough to allow the desired level of exports. The only constraint on growth is that imposed by the maximum feasible domestic savings.

The second view stresses that many goods have strategic importance for growth but cannot be produced domestically at early stages of development and have to be imported. It questions the capacity of certain poor countries to freely export their domestic output either because of international demand conditions (with restricted access to markets in the developed countries and inelastic foreign demand curves) or because of domestic supply conditions at low levels of economic development. Bottlenecks may, therefore, arise because of inadequate supplies of certain foreign goods. The maximum potential domestic savings of a poor economy may not be fully used for capital formation and the dominant constraint on growth will be availability of foreign exchange. Foreign assistance in this context is required primarily not to supplement domestic savings but to relieve the import constraint on growth. When this bottleneck constraint holds, foreign assistance will have a greater effect on the growth rate than if the savings constraint is binding.

Hence two separable constraints on growth – savings and imports – are identified. The contribution to economic growth of a given flow of foreign assistance will differ depending on which is the binding constraint in an economy.[3]

32

Alternatively, the requirements of foreign assistance to achieve a *given* growth rate in an economy will vary according to which constraint is considered the dominant one. (This issue is considered in the next chapter.)

Let us now consider a simple model of an economy receiving no foreign capital where the dominant constraint on growth, in one case, is set by the maximum feasible savings rate and, in the other case, by the maximum import (export) rate. It is then possible to show the differential effect of foreign capital assistance on the growth rate.

It is initially assumed that the only imports are capital goods which the economy, at an early stage of development, does not have the physical capacity or skills to produce domestically. The income (Y) of the economy is assumed to grow at the same rate as its output potential (P) because there is assumed to be full utilization of available capacity.

Assume the economy has the following type of aggregate production function where K_d and K_m represent imports of domestic and foreign capital goods respectively which are required in fixed proportions.

$$P = \min (\alpha \, K_d, \, B \, K_m) \qquad (1)$$

This notation means that output is given by whichever bracketed expression yields the smallest value. The units for capital goods are such that one unit of output capacity (P) can be used to construct one unit of K_d or exchange for one unit of K_m at fixed terms of trade (i.e. the price of all the inputs and outputs is one).

To increase the potential output of the economy requires net investment expenditure on domestic and foreign capital goods and the level of investment (I) is determined by the propensity to save (s) and current income. The extra output obtained from a unit of investment $\left(\dfrac{dY}{I} \right)$ and therefore the growth rate made possible by a given savings rate (s) will depend on whether there are any constraints on the

33

availability of the two inputs – domestic and foreign capital goods, other than that set by availability of savings.

Savings limited growth

We may assume that units of domestic output are freely convertible into foreign capital goods, because the export capabilities of the economy are sufficient to finance the required imported capital goods arising from the investment level. In this case the growth rate will be constrained only by the domestic savings rate (s). This is the usual assumption of the Harrod-Domar type models.

The growth rate of the economy is given by δs where δ is the output/investment ratio. What is the value of δ given the above production function?

Since there is no constraint on either input (other than that set by available investible resources) foreign and domestic capital goods can be combined in the appropriate proportions. The extra output arising from a unit of investment

$$(\text{saving}) = \frac{dP}{I} = \frac{dY}{I} = \delta = \frac{B\alpha}{B + \alpha} \quad ^4 \qquad (2)$$

Trade limited growth

However, if the export capabilities of the economy are not sufficient to finance the required imported capital goods then the growth rate δs will not be achieved and a foreign exchange bottleneck will exist.

Suppose that maximum possible exports are a constant proportion (x) of domestic output (Y). Then, the maximum possible rate of growth of the economy, whatever the savings rate, will be Bx. This follows from the nature of the production function assumed in the earlier section, since x represents the maximum proportion of output which can be converted into imported capital goods (K_m). If $Bx < \delta s$, a

34

bottleneck exists which prevents the economy growing at the rate suggested by the domestic savings constraint. Potential savings are frustrated in this case because there is an inadequate supply of imported capital goods.

This is a plausible situation in certain developing countries where exports are a small proportion of domestic output; where there may be difficulties in raising the export rate, and where the imported capital goods input per unit of output may be large because the economy has not developed a diversified industrial production structure.[5]

Now consider the effects of an inflow of foreign capital (F) on the growth rate of the economy. Let $f = \dfrac{F}{Y}$ be the rate of capital inflow.

If a *savings* constraint exists, f has the effect of supplementing s or increasing the level of investment in both domestic and imported capital goods. The growth rate with capital assistance will then be:

$$\delta (s + f) \qquad (3)$$

If an *import* constraint is dominant, f has the effect of supplementing x, the capacity to import capital goods. The growth rate with capital assistance will then be:

$$B (x + f) \qquad (4)$$

If production requires input of *both* domestic and imported capital goods, then B must be greater than δ. This follows mathematically.[6] Hence a given inflow of foreign aid (f) will have a greater effect on the growth rate if there is an import constraint which overrides the savings constraint in an economy. This is illustrated in Figure 1 when initially with no aid $Bx < \delta s$, the effect of a capital inflow on the growth rate is given by the line with slope equal to B up to the point Q, where the savings constrained growth rate operates again. From this point onwards the effect of aid on growth is given by the line with the lower slope (δ).

Figure 1 *Effect of capital inflow on growth rate*

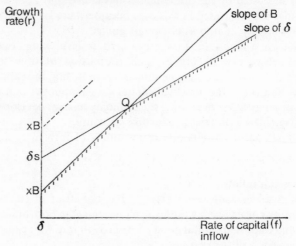

Thus, although a dominating import constraint depresses the growth rate below that made possible by its potential savings rate, a given inflow of foreign aid to relieve this bottleneck has a greater effect on growth because it activates otherwise unusable domestic savings. Thus foreign savings (or foreign capital) is always as good as domestic savings but in certain conditions is better than domestic savings because it augments foreign exchange (and hence imported capital goods) also.

Aid for current imports

As well as capital goods imports, a poor economy may require imports of raw material and components for maintaining and replacing existing capital goods as well as consumer goods. If exports are not adequate to finance import needs of this kind, no growth will be possible. Some foreign capital would be necessary in this case to ensure that the economy was operating at the full capacity level of output. The rate of growth made possible by foreign aid (in excess of that needed to ensure adequate current imports) will depend on whether or not imported capital goods are also required for domestic production.

Let us take the case where both current and capital goods imports are required for production. Let the production function of the economy, as before, take the form:

$$P = \min (\alpha K_d, \ BK_m, \ mM) \text{ where } B > 0, \alpha > 0, m > 1$$
(5)

It is assumed that the value of output exceeds the value of imported current inputs (M) so that m is greater than unity. If the maximum export rate of the economy (x) is inadequate to sustain the necessary current imports, capital transfers (f) will have to exceed $\dfrac{1}{m} - x$ for any growth of capacity to occur at all. In other words, a foreign aid transfer will not release a bottleneck (import) on growth unless it is more than adequate to finance the uncovered current import needs of the economy. If foreign aid exceeds the current import gap $\left(\text{i.e. } f > \dfrac{1}{m} - x\right)$ then the economy will grow at a rate $B\left(x + f - \dfrac{1}{m}\right)$. See Figure 2. For aid flows over and above current import needs the impact on the growth rate will be determined by the value of B. It should be noted in this case, that only the proportion of domestic output (P) which is net of imported current inputs (i.e. $P\left(1 - \dfrac{1}{m}\right)$) is available for domestic consumption and capital formation. The savings propensity out of net output must be large enough to ensure that s, the savings rate, is the same as in the case where no imported current inputs are required.

Suppose, now, to take a more extreme case, an economy had developed an advanced domestic capital goods industry

37

so that no *foreign* capital goods were required for production, but its export capability was not adequate to finance the required current imports to ensure full utilization of its

Figure 2   Effect of capital inflow on growth rate

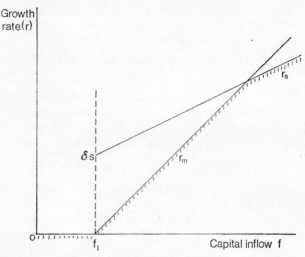

r_m (rate of growth with import constraint)
$$= B\left(x + f - \frac{1}{m}\right)$$

r_s (rate of growth with savings constraint)
$$= \delta(f + s)$$
$$f_1 = \frac{1}{m} - x \text{ where } \frac{1}{m} > x$$

domestic productive capacity. (This is not unlike the situation which confronted India in the early 1960s. India, of course, required imported capital goods but the pressing problem was its inability to finance large enough 'maintenance' import requirements.) Foreign capital which fills *some* of the gap between export earnings and current import needs would) of course, raise utilization of existing capacity but it would not permit any growth of capacity. If f was less than $\left(\dfrac{1}{m} - x\right)$ it would affect the level of output (income) but not the *growth* rate.

However, if the aid flows are adequate to fill the whole of the current import gap it would have an effect on growth. In terms of Figure 2, if the rate of capital inflow were less than f_1 no growth would occur. Beyond the critical level of f_1 aid, growth will occur at a rate r_m constrained by foreign exchange availability.

The analysis suggests that aid can be 'developmental' or growth permitting, even if it does not finance the import of capital goods. Assistance for financing adequate imports of current materials inputs in this situation permits growth of output. It enables a country to effectively use its existing capacity as well as its domestic savings potential to add to capacity. Of course, even if aid is not adequate to permit capital accumulation it is still justifiable as a 'rescue operation' to relieve the current import constraint and allow fuller utilization of its existing capacity until the export rate can be raised.

The role of aid in the labour surplus economy

So far we have ignored labour inputs in production on the assumption that the supply of unskilled labour does not constrain growth in most poor countries. The main constraints are maximum feasible domestic savings, rates or availability of imported capital and current materials. However, let us suppose that foreign capital goods and materials are not required for production and further that investment in domestic capital goods only requires labour. In this case it would appear that in a surplus-labour economy, capital accumulation could proceed using idle labour without any domestic saving or import constraint; provided labour is transferred from agriculture (say) where its marginal product is zero, to work on capital construction at the same real wage as before, and provided those remaining in agriculture do not consume any extra goods after the departure of their colleagues, there appears to be no limit on capital accumulation while idle labour exists and no need for foreign capital inflows. However, if we ignore the unreality of the production function assumptions, there is an important reason why labour-intensive investment may be limited. Institutionally, there is a problem in most poor countries in preventing a net increase in consumption when idle labour is transferred into investment activity. It is politically difficult (*via* taxes, etc.) to prevent a rise in consumption *per capita* in the agricultural sector from which the idle labour is normally drawn. In this case consumer goods cannot be released beyond a certain point for feeding the newly employed workers. This institutional constraint on extra capital formation can be relieved if a foreign capital inflow permits the import of extra consumer goods (mainly food) required by the investment workers. Aid in this case not only permits a fuller utilization of the productive potential of labour in the economy, it also allows a higher rate of capital formation. Food aid which can often be justified as a 'relief' measure would in this context permit greater capital formation.[7]

Aid and self-sustained growth

If a positive rate of aid flow (aid as proportion of G.N.P.) is necessary for achieving the desired growth rate, the above model has the implication that aid transfer in *absolute* terms must rise continuously over time. This follows from the assumptions of the model; that savings and export propensities are constant, that possibilities of import substitution are ignored and that there are fixed coefficients between production inputs. When these assumptions are relaxed, the possibility that aid transfers can eventually be phased out emerges, so that aid can be viewed as a 'pump priming' instrument which ultimately permits self-sustained growth. It is possible to spell out the conditions necessary to ensure that the specified growth rate ultimately becomes self-supporting for any particular economy. This is an important calculation because neither donors or recipients find the prospect of continuously rising aid flows attractive.

There are clearly many possible configurations of structural changes which could eventually ensure self-sustaining growth. Two simple cases may be considered, assuming first, a savings constraint, and, second, a trade constraint on growth, but assuming that the production function remains unchanged.

Savings constraint only

Consider an economy in which there are no export limitations on growth but only a domestic savings constraint. Initially the domestic savings rate is too low to permit the desired growth rate without foreign assistance but the required foreign capital is provided. What must be the nature of the domestic savings function if the desired growth rate is to be achieved but foreign aid injections are to fall to zero over a finite period?

Let

The target growth rate $= \bar{r}$
Incremental output/capital ratio $= \delta$
Then the required investment rate $= \dfrac{\bar{r}}{\delta}$

Also let the *absolute* level of income, investment, domestic savings and foreign assistance be Y_t, I_t, S_t and F_t respectively.

In $t = 0$, investment $I_0 = \dfrac{\bar{r}}{\delta} \cdot Y_0$ and savings $S_0 = \dfrac{\bar{r}}{\delta} \cdot Y_0 - F_0$, since foreign aid is initially positive to ensure the required investment.

Income grows at rate $\bar{r}$, so

$$Y_t = Y_0(1 + \bar{r})^t \tag{6}$$

$$I_t = \frac{\bar{r}}{\delta} Y_t \tag{7}$$

$$S_t = \left(\frac{\bar{r}}{\delta} Y_0 - F_0\right) + \bar{s}(Y_t - Y_0) \tag{8}$$

where $\bar{s} = $ marginal domestic savings rate.

Hence foreign assistance in year $t = F_t = I_t - S_t$

$$= \left(\frac{\bar{r}}{\delta} - \bar{s}\right)(Y_t - Y_0) + F_0, (F_0 > 0) \tag{9}$$

For F_t to decline $\bar{s} \geqslant \frac{\bar{r}}{\delta}$.

In words, for self-sustaining growth to be achieved the *marginal* domestic savings rate must exceed the required investment rate. Otherwise the maintenance of the growth rate, $\bar{r}$, would require increasing injections of foreign aid over time. The more $\bar{s}$ exceeds $\frac{\bar{r}}{\delta}$, the more quickly will foreign aid be phased out in the absence of other structural changes in the aided economy.

The prospects for self-sustained growth

Does the performance of developing countries in recent years appear to satisfy the savings criterion for self-sustained growth? The criteria in terms of this model are that empirically the average domestic savings rate (s) or the marginal domestic savings rate ($\bar{s}$) should be equal to, or exceed, the investment rate required to maintain a satisfactory target rate of growth of G.N.P. ($\bar{r}$) $\left(\text{i.e. } s \geqslant \frac{\bar{r}}{\delta} \text{ or } \bar{s} \geqslant \frac{\bar{r}}{\delta} \right)$.

If it is assumed that 0.05[8] represents a satisfactory minimum rate of growth ($\bar{r}$) for all developing countries, then the desired investment rate for each country can be calculated using values for the output–capital ratio (δ) which have been recorded in these countries in a recent period.

Table 6 sets out data for 31 developing countries which refer to the period 1957–62. In so far as recorded performance in this short period is a true indication of each country's

Table 6 Performance of developing countries 1957–62
It is assumed that the desired rate of growth of all these countries ($\bar{r}$) is 0·05. The 'savings' conditions for self-sustained growth are that $S > \dfrac{\bar{r}}{\delta}$ or $S > \dfrac{\bar{r}}{\delta}$.

| Country | Capital inflow 1962 (F/Y) | Required investment rate $\left(\dfrac{\bar{r}}{\delta}\right)$ | Actual savings performance | | Actual growth rate (G.N.P.) 1957–62 |
			Average rate (s) 1962	Marginal rate (s̄) 1957–62	
A *Countries meeting the saving criteria*					
Burma	0·00	0·205	0·17	0·21	0·046
Israel	0·20	0·154	0·11	0·15	0·103
Jordan	0·24	0·068	−0·07	0·09	0·111
Korea	0·10	0·172	0·03	0·27	0·040
Malaya	−0·04	0·116	0·22	0·26	0·062
Pakistan	0·04	0·117	0·09	0·25	0·041
Panama	0·06	0·156	0·12	0·37	0·051
Peru	−0·01	0·155	0·21	0·31	0·073
Philippines	0·02	0·139	0·12	0·30	0·050
Taiwan	0·07	0·134	0·15	0·29	0·074
Thailand	0·01	0·106	0·16	0·22	0·080
Trinidad– Tobago	0·10	0·217	0·22	0·11	0·078
Argentina	0·03	0·533	0·21	0·83	0·019
Brazil	0·03	0·132	0·15	0·19	0·067
Greece	0·06	0·151	0·15	0·26	0·060
Honduras	−0·01	0·203	0·13	0·25	0·033
India	0·02	0·145	0·12	0·20	0·048
Nigeria	0·05	0·185	0·09	0·19	0·033
B *Countries not meeting the saving criteria*					
Iran	0·01	0·177	0·14	0·11	0·049
Mexico	0·01	0·153	0·13	0·11	0·050
Venezuela	−0·06	0·326	0·27	−0·26	0·043
Bolivia	0·07	0·216	0·04	−0·16	0·029
Chile	0·06	0·138	0·07	0·10	0·038
Colombia	0·04	0·208	0·16	−0·12	0·050
Costa Rica	0·05	0·236	0·11	−0·10	0·039
Guatemala	0·02	0·176	0·08	−0·03	0·036
Liberia	0·56	0·390	0·11	0·21	0·046
Mauritius	0·09	0·249	0·10	−0·39	0·034
Paraguay	0·03	0·318	0·13	0·08	0·026
Tunisia	0·18	0·245	0·08	−0·84	0·034
Turkey	0·03	0·240	0·12	−0·02	0·030

Source: Data derived from H. Chenery and A. Strout, 'Foreign Assistance and Economic Development', *American Economic Review*, September 1966, Table 6.

future savings capabilities, it may be concluded that 18 of the 31 countries satisfy the saving condition for self-sustained growth. Not all of these countries were receiving foreign assistance in 1962; of the 26 receiving aid, 14 satisfied this test.

However, recent statistical evidence on the magnitude of saving and other parameters may be very misleading for prediction – an issue which is discussed in the next chapter. For this reason an alternative approach to the estimation of long-run domestic savings behaviour in developing countries may yield a more reliable assessment of their capacity for ultimately self-sustained growth.

Over time as income grows, the incomes *not* likely to be available for investment are composed of three main elements: (*a*) the increase in income required to support the increase in population; (*b*) the increase in income which must be earmarked for consumption to provide incentives for growth or to meet rising expectations; (*c*) the increase in domestic production lost through deterioration in the terms of trade.

Looked at in this way, the prospects for the aided countries do not appear as optimistic as the Table 6 data on marginal savings suggest. Thus, for the aided countries in Section A of Table 6, the average saving rate in 1962 was typically 0·10 and required investment rate typically 0·16. If their population growth is 0·03 and the 'incentive' increase in consumption is 0·02 per annum (no allowance for terms of trade deterioration), then with a G.N.P. growth rate of 0·05 the marginal savings rate would be no higher than the 1962 average rate and well below the required investment rate. Of course, population growth is not always as high as this and it is possible for governments to hold down increases in consumption as incomes rise (for short periods at least).

Time period for self-sustained growth

One of the strategies for allocation of aid among developing countries is that it should be concentrated on those countries likely to achieve independence of external assistance within a given period of time.[9] How long will it take a country to achieve self-sustained growth and how much assistance will be required?

Clearly this problem can be answered in terms of the savings constraint model outlined above, provided empirical values can be given to the main parameters.

Given a target rate of growth ($\bar{r}$) the value of the output–capital ratio and the initial domestic savings rate, the time required for an economy to achieve self-sustained growth at rate $\bar{r}$, will depend (in the savings constraint model) on the marginal savings rate ($\bar{s}$). This is intuitively obvious and the following figures for $\bar{t}$ (years to independence of external assistance) indicate its sensitivity to $\bar{s}$.

$\bar{s}$	$\bar{t}$
	(*years*)
0·20	α
0·22	40
0·25	27
0·30	18
0·40	14

This calculation makes the assumptions that

1   the growth rate is 0·06, output–capital ratio is 0·3 and the initial domestic savings rate is zero.
2   the magnitude of the marginal savings rate will remain constant for the whole period $\bar{t}$.
3   that capital transfers are entirely in grant form so there is no debt service which would otherwise prolong the period of time required to become completely independent of foreign assistance.

It is noticeable that for marginal savings rates within empirically plausible limits (0·10 to 0·30), the time period is extremely sensitive to the actual savings rate.

Export constraint

Growth at the desired rate may be constrained by lack of export capability rather than domestic savings. In this case what condition is required to ensure that aid flows to supplement export earnings initially, will eventually fall to zero?

Suppose only capital goods are imported but exports initially are inadequate to finance the required level of imported capital goods to achieve the desired growth rate. By a similar analysis to that in the previous section it can be shown that growth will eventually be sustained by the country's own export earnings if the marginal export propensity $x > \dfrac{\bar{r}}{B}$.[10]

It is not easy to test this condition empirically because most poor countries import current inputs as well as capital goods and the value of B is difficult to ascertain.

The greater the extent to which $\bar{x}$ exceeds the $\dfrac{\bar{r}}{B}$ ratio, the faster will self-sustained growth be achieved and the smaller the total aid transfer required.

Skill constraints

The preceding analysis has assumed that there are no domestic institutional limits on the achievement of the desired growth rate other than savings and export potentiality. In practice, however, growth depends heavily on the availability of skilled workers, managers, technical personnel and civil servants. The lack of these skills can severely limit the amount of productive investment which can be planned, organized and executed and sets what is commonly called the 'absorptive capacity' of an economy.

One treatment of skill shortages would be to postulate various skill/output coefficients where skills are seen as inputs in a production function in the same way as domestic and imported capital goods. Alternatively, skill availability can be viewed as a function of the development of an economy, independent of its capacity to save or import. In this case it is possible to postulate a limit on the 'ability to invest' productively.

In the early phases of development many economies may not have the managerial, organizational and technical skills and experience to achieve the level of investment which their domestic savings (plus foreign capital) would otherwise permit. This constraint on the ability to invest may limit an economy's absorptive capacity for foreign capital and its growth rate. The absorptive capacity can however be raised and the extent to which this can be done is partly a function of savings and external resources and partly a function of time.

Skills can be augmented by investing in the education and training of people and this requires savings. Skills can also be increased by importing foreign personnel to use directly or indirectly in training local people. Foreign assistance can finance both and hence can relieve skill bottlenecks. However, the human capabilities of an economy are very much a function of *time*, because the ability to carry out an investment programme *effectively* is largely a matter of 'learning by doing'. It is the passage of time and the speed of the development process which is likely to set the important and overriding limit on the absorptive capacity of an economy for capital.

It has therefore been suggested that the ability to invest effectively may be most plausibly represented by the maximum rate of growth of investment over time where investment is measured in absolute terms.

This view can be set out formally as follows where q represents the maximum growth rate of investment over time set by skills and experience.[11] It is assumed for simplicity to be a constant.

47

(i) Ability to invest $\quad I_t = I_0(1 + q)^t \qquad (10)$

(ii) Savings constraint $\quad S_t = S_0 + \bar{s}(Y_t - Y_0) \qquad (11)$

(iii) Incremental output/capital ratio

$$\delta = \frac{dY}{I}$$

Foreign assistance $F_t = I_t - S_t$. Hence solving for the level of foreign assistance which can be used for investment gives

$$F_t = \left(\frac{q}{\delta} - \bar{s}\right)(Y_t - Y_0) + F_0, \text{ where } F_0 = I_0 - S_0$$

$$(12)$$

By comparing this equation with equations (6) and (9) above it is clear that if q is less than $\delta(s + f)$ or $B(x + f)$ then there is a 'skill determined' limit on growth which overrides the other constraints. This lowers the rate of growth and puts a limit on the inflow of foreign capital (f) which can be effectively used.

Some economies may well be in this early phase of skill-limited development. In this situation the increased flow of foreign assistance ($F_t - F_0$) finances the difference between the increment of investment permitted by skills and the increment of domestic savings.

At the end of this skill dominated phase of development the rate of increase of investment will drop to $\bar{r}$ and foreign aid flows to achieve $\bar{r}$ will be determined by the savings or import constraints on growth.

Conclusion

The main conclusions of this chapter are that, apart from skills, there are two separable constraints on growth – savings and foreign exchange. Hence an increment of foreign assistance may have a different effect on growth from an increment of domestic savings. These conclusions follow logically from the assumptions of the model used. The crucial assumptions are (*a*) that exports are a fixed proportion of domestic income and (*b*) that imported inputs are essential for domestic production and the aggregate production function has fixed coefficients.

The plausibility of these conclusions therefore depend on whether these are plausible technological and economic assumptions to make in the context of most developing countries. Whether such extreme lack of substitutability between domestic and foreign resources exists is an empirical question and the next chapter is concerned with attempting an answer to this question.

Notes

1   It will not be necessary at this stage to specify an adequate growth rate for a poor country, but this will need to be done when calculating foreign capital requirements for development in the following chapter. An adequate growth rate might be defined as one which would permit the minimum growth in output *per capita* consistent with political and social stability, and it would depend on the growth of population and how rapidly aspirations are growing.

2   Effects of skill limitations will be considered later.

3   An evaluation of the second view is provided in Ch. 4 below. This is sometimes termed the 'structuralist' view. The rest of the analysis in this chapter accepts that there are two separable constraints on growth.

4   In this case, a unit of investment will be expended on K_m and K_d in the proportions $\dfrac{\alpha}{B + \alpha}$ and $\dfrac{B}{B + \alpha}$ respectively. This follows because $\alpha K_d \equiv B K_m$ and $(K_d + K_m) = 1$. The extra output given by one unit of investment is then $= \dfrac{B\alpha}{B + \alpha}$.

5   The assumptions of fixed production coefficients and fixed export rates are crucial in the above analysis and their economic plausibility is questioned in the next chapter.

6   It has been shown that

$$\delta = \frac{\alpha B}{\alpha + B} \quad \therefore \ \delta(\alpha + B) = \alpha B \quad \therefore \ \alpha\delta = \alpha B - \delta B$$

$$\therefore \ B = \frac{\delta}{1 - \delta/\alpha}$$

But $\delta/\alpha > 0 < 1$ $(\alpha > 0,\ B > 0)$ so $B > \delta$.

7 'Relief' food aid is required to prevent an unacceptable *decline* in food consumption per head when domestic food output is disrupted.

8 This is an arbitrary value but one which would ensure that *per capita* income would double in 50 years with a population growth rate of 0·03.

9 See Ch. 2.

10 Foreign assistance (F_t) for growth rate $(\bar{r}) = M_t - X_t$

where M_t = imported capital goods

X_t = exports

$M_t = \dfrac{r}{B} Y_t$, and $X_t = X_0 + \bar{x}(Y_t - Y_0)$ where $\bar{x}$ = marginal propensity to export.

Hence $F_t = \left(\dfrac{\bar{r}}{B} - \bar{x}\right) Y_t + \bar{x}Y_0 - X_0$. F_t will decline if $\bar{x} > \dfrac{r}{B}$.

11 In economic theory, the appropriate level of investment is usually assessed in relation to a schedule of the marginal efficiency of investment or the marginal rate of return. To specify a rigid limit to the scale of feasible investment, as is done here, implies that on an investment schedule the rate of return would drop, at some point, sharply to zero.

4

Aid and economic growth II

The model outlined in the last chapter can clearly form the basis of a methodology for empirical estimation of the level of foreign assistance required to achieve growth targets in developing economies, individually or as a whole. Ignoring skill constraints this model implies that two resource gaps – a 'savings' gap and a 'trade' gap – need to be estimated. It further implies that these two gaps need not be identical and that foreign capital must be adequate to fill the larger gap if the planned growth rate is to materialize. Two-gap computable models of this kind have been used in practice to estimate aid requirements of developing countries[1] (see Table 7).

It is the economic theory underlying this methodology of foreign resource needs which must now be clarified and examined.

Ex-ante and ex-post concepts

The first point to clarify is the distinction between *ex-ante* and *ex-post* magnitudes of the resource gaps. In an *ex-post* or accounting sense the two resource gaps are identical; it is only when the savings and foreign exchange gaps are viewed in an *ex-ante* or planned sense that they may differ.

E   51

The *ex-post* or accounting identity of two resource gaps is an elementary formal proposition and can be demonstrated as follows: Goods and services which are put to use in an economy come from two sources, home production (Y) and imports of goods and services (M). These are used for consumption (C), investment (I) and exports of goods and services (X) where C and I include imported consumer goods and investment goods.

Hence,

(i) $Y + M \equiv C + I + X$
   or $Y \equiv C + I + X - M$

Domestic production (Y) gives rise to incomes which are identical to the total value of production[2] and this income is spent on consumer goods (C) or saved (S) so that

(ii) $Y = C + S$
   From (i) and (ii) it can be seen that C is common to both sides of the equation and the equation can be rearranged as

(iii) $I = S + M - X$
   This indicates that $M - X$ is the excess of imports of goods and services over exports, or the deficit (or surplus) on the current account of a country's balance of payments. This must be identical with the net capital inflow (F), defined to include any net change in the external reserves of the economy. Thus

(iv) $M - X \equiv F$
   When (iii) is rearranged we have
   $I - S \equiv M - X \equiv F$

It is clear that the net inflow of foreign capital plays a dual role but in the accounting sense the savings gap is identical with the trade gap.

Long-run ex-ante resource gaps

However, this necessary identity arises after the event (*ex post*) when it is possible to look back retrospectively at what happened. *Ex ante*, looking forward, the resource gaps may differ because, in the long run, those who make the decisions about saving, investing, importing and exporting are not always the same people and they are not all affected by the same factors. The situation can be illustrated by Figure 3 which relates the two *ex-ante* gaps or required levels of net foreign capital inflow (F) to different target growth rates of income $(\bar{r})$. The $X - M$ schedule represents the *ex-ante* export–import gap in any particular period 't' for various growth rates. The $I - S$ schedule, similarly, represents the *ex-ante* savings gap in period 't'.

The particular *ex-ante* schedules of Figure 3 are based on the following five equations which correspond closely to the type of model outlined in the last chapter.

$$Y_t = Y_0(1 + \bar{r})^t$$

$$I_t = \frac{\bar{r}}{\delta} Y_t$$

$$S_t = S_0 + \bar{s}(Y_t - Y_0)$$

$$M_t = M_0 + \bar{m}(Y_t - Y_0)$$

$$X_t = X_0(1 + x)^t$$

where $\bar{m}$ is the minimum marginal propensity to import and x is the maximum anticipated rate of growth of exports which is assumed to be *exogenously* determined.[3] The other variables have already been defined in the last chapter. The *ex-ante* gap is measured either by $I_t - S_t$ or $M_t - X_t$ and these are both a function of the growth rate $(\bar{r})$, given the initial values of income, saving, exports and imports and the exogenously determined rate of growth of exports (x).

It must be stressed at this stage that the assumed functional relationships are somewhat unorthodox. Both investment and saving are uniquely determined by the level of income

53

and no other factors. Imports (M_t) are assumed to be the *minimum consistent* with a given income level so that $\bar{m}$ represents the marginal 'necessity' to import. While, for exports, x represents the *maximum possible* rate of growth over time. It follows that there are two unique and independent schedules relating the $I - S$ gap and the $M - X$ gap to various growth rates.

These functions are unorthodox in not including a *price* variable explicitly.[4] This implies that either prices are assumed to be inflexible or that, with price flexibility, demand and supply conditions for exports and imports (for example) are such that no price changes would alter export earnings or import payments at a given level of income. These implicit and somewhat restrictive assumptions are reconsidered later but if accepted it is quite possible to have two independent schedules as in Figure 3.

At Q in Figure 3 both *ex-ante* gaps are equal (OF_0). If

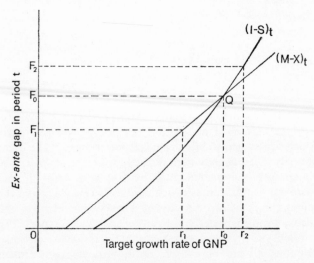

Figure 3 Ex-ante *'saving' and 'trade' gaps and growth rates*

54

the target growth rate happened to be r_0, then this rate of growth would be achieved if net foreign capital inflow of OF_0 were actually forthcoming.[5] However, suppose the target growth rate is r_1 then the trade gap is larger than the savings gap, *ex ante*. If foreign capital is not adequate to fill the larger gap (OF_1) this growth rate will not be achieved. Short-run forces will bring about *ex-post* equality of the two gaps but at the expense of frustrating the growth target. Similarly if the target rate is r_2, capital inflow must meet the larger savings gap (OF_2). On the basis of this basic methodology several estimates have been made of *ex-ante* aid requirements of individual developing countries and developing countries as a whole. Table 7 sets out some of these, distinguishing those based respectively on 'savings' and 'trade' gaps. The Appendix discusses statistical problems in estimation of these gaps.

Evaluation of the dual gap hypothesis

One crucial assumption of the 'dual constraint' or 'dual gap' model must now be examined. The model set out in the last chapter shows that an increment of foreign assistance can have a different effect on growth from an increment of domestic savings. This follows from the assumption that there is inadequate scope for substitution between domestic and foreign resources. More specifically, two main rigidities are built into the models, viz.,

a that there is a limit on the scope for expanding export earnings because of inelasticities of either foreign demand or domestic supply and
b that imported inputs are essential for production and the aggregate production function assumes fixed input coefficients.

With these rigidities the *ex-ante* $M - X$ gap may diverge from the *ex-ante* $I - S$ gap. Export earnings are inexpandable and imports incompressible beyond a certain level. The

55

Table 7 Estimates of aggregate savings and trade gaps of developing countries

A Savings gap (billion $)

Source	Period of projection	Growth rate of G.N.P. per capita (%)	Capital-output coefficient	Required annual capital inflow
U.N.[1] (1949)	1950–60	2·0	5·8	8·5
Millikan/Rostow[2] (1953)	—	2·0	3·0	6·5
Hoffmann[3] (1959)	1960–9	2·0	3·0	7·0
Rosenstein-Rodan[4] (1961)	1962–6	1·8	2·8	6·4
	1967–71	2·2	2·8	6·4
	1971–6	2·5	2·8	5·0
UNCTAD (1968)	1975 (L)			3·6
	1975 (H)			7·6

B Trade gap (billion $)

Source	Year of projection	Imports	Exports	Trade gap	Debt service gap	Foreign exchange gap
U.N.[5]	1970	41·0	29·0	12·0	8·0	20·0
G. Blau[6]	1970	41·0	31·0	10·0	8·0	18·0
B. Belassa[7]	1970	38·0	33·0	5·0	5·5	10·5
	1975	49·0	42·0	7·0	6·9	13·7
UNCTAD[8]	1975 (L)					12·5
	1975 (H)					17·6

[1] *U.N. Measures for Economic Development* 1949. [2] M. Millikan & W. Rostow, *A Proposal: Key to Effective Foreign Policy*, 1956. [3] P. G. Hoffmann, *One hundred Countries*, 1960. [4] P. Rosenstein-Rodan, *Review of Economics & Statistics*, May 1961. [5] *U.N. World Economic Survey 1962.* [6] G. Blau, *Commodity Export Earnings & Economic Growth*, 1963. [7] B. Belassa, *Problem of Growth in less developed Economies* (O.E.C.D.), 1963. [8] UNCTAD, *Trade Prospects & Capital Needs of Developing Countries*, 1968. These estimates at 1960 prices refer to the sum of the gaps in Asian and Latin American countries. A high and a low estimate is given.

'trade' gap may then exceed the 'savings' gap and unless foreign assistance fills the larger gap the target growth rate will not be achieved.

Why should these rigidities be assumed to reflect the situation in developing countries?

The view of some economists is that there are 'structural' factors which create these rigidities in developing countries. Policy measures such as changes in domestic prices or exchange rates in these countries will not be effective in altering export earnings or import payments at a given level of domestic incomes or outputs. Thus a unity elasticity of foreign demand for exports or the lack of any effective domestic substitute for certain imported goods used in the production process would constitute structural rigidities.

The alternative and more traditional view is that there are unlikely to be such rigidities if prices are flexible. If resources are optimally allocated there can only be one constraint (savings) on growth and one *ex-ante* resource gap (savings). If appropriate price policies or exchange rates policies are followed, resources would be switched to eliminate the difference between the growth effect of imports and domestic saving and hence the difference in the *ex-ante* gaps. On this view, if a dominating *ex-ante* trade gap exists it indicates current or past misallocation of resources and must be the result of inappropriate price policies.

To illustrate the difference between these two views consider an economy where *all* capital goods are imported (and only capital goods are imported) and where all exports are consumer goods. With these assumptions, to save means to export and to invest means to import.

Consider exports first and postulate a foreign demand curve, a domestic demand curve and a domestic supply curve for a typical export (consumer good) as in Figure 4. First, assume that the foreign demand curve is perfectly elastic (F_1F_1). In this case, an increase in saving will shift the domestic demand curve (D_1D_1) leftward to D_2D_2. The

REED LIBRARY
STATE UNIVERSITY COLLEGE
FREDONIA, NEW YORK 14063

57

quantity of consumer goods consumed at home falls by the same amount (*ab*) as exports increase and hence permits an equivalent import of capital goods.[6] The trade constraint and the saving constraint on capital formation are identical.

However, suppose the foreign demand curve for exports to have unity elasticity or to be kinked such that it is inelastic for a fall in price and elastic for a rise in price. In this case it is clear that an increase in saving cannot increase the value of exports. This type of rigidity is 'structural' in the sense that a domestic policy change in the economy, such as devaluation, cannot break the bottleneck on foreign exchange. In this simple economy where only consumer goods are exported and only capital goods imported, this outcome seems to require that foreign demand curves be of this kind for *all* goods produced by the economy. Are these plausible conditions to assume for developing countries? Taking developing countries as a whole, and certain primary products, international demand curves may approximate to unity elasticity. For individual countries which have a monopolistic position in the international market (e.g. Pakistan jute) demand conditions may be of this kind. Also, where international agreements and market sharing arrangements exist, a kinked demand curve may exist for the individual supplier. However, it is implausible to assume that these demand conditions face all primary products and all individual country suppliers.

In the case of manufactures (*vis-à-vis* primary products) the aggregate and individual demand curves for developing countries are likely to be highly elastic with respect to price except where these manufactures face quantitative restrictions on their entry into the markets of developed countries.[7]

There may, however, be a supply problem with exports from a developing country even if demand is elastic. Domestic market protection of industries may have created a cost structure which makes them internationally uncompetitive. Thus in Figure 4 the supply curve of exports may be S_1S_2

where domestic suppliers are unwilling to export at all whatever the shift in domestic demand (increase in savings). This, however, may reflect an overvaluation of the domestic currency and a devaluation would normally raise the foreign curve (in domestic currency) to say F_2F_2 in Figure 4 and

Figure 4   Demand and supply of exports

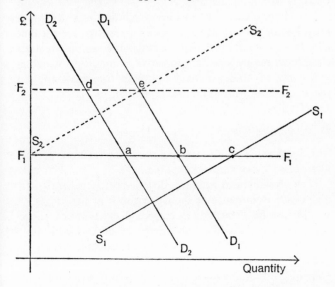

induce exports of *de* when savings increase. In this case there would appear to be no structural rigidity if the appropriate price policies were pursued. Moreover, if primary products face a unity elasticity of demand and manufactures face an elastic demand, then differential effective exchange rate changes would permit a net expansion of export earnings.

What about imports? A structural problem would mean that it is impossible, by changing relative prices, to reduce imports without lowering the level of domestic output.

59

In the simple economy where all capital goods are imported and only consumer goods produced domestically, a structural problem implies that (*a*) in production no substitution between imported capital goods and domestic factors is possible and (*b*) in consumption no substitution between different consumer goods is possible.[8] Although for certain products and processes rigidities of this kind exist, they are unlikely to hold generally.

The simplifications of this approach and its static nature must be borne in mind but it does suggest that the existence of a trade constraint which overrides the saving constraint on growth requires rather restrictive assumptions which are not likely to hold generally although they may apply to particular countries at a particular time.[9]

Policy implications

The long-run and short-run policy implications of these alternative views are considerable.

If these structural rigidities do not prevail generally then an *ex-ante* dominance of the trade gap over the saving gap would not be expected. If empirical calculations suggest that this pattern is likely to emerge generally (see Table 7) then an important long-run variable, relative prices, has probably been left out of the formulation. Indeed, the existence of a dominant *ex-ante* trade gap may well reflect past and present misallocation of resources due to faulty pricing policies. Instead of using foreign assistance to fill the *difference* between the 'saving' gap and the larger 'trade' gap, a change in prices would perform this function. The establishment of an equilibrium exchange rate would alter relative home and foreign prices and help to reallocate resources in the economy from serving domestic to serving foreign demand and from import-using to import-saving activities. Foreign assistance would still be required to meet a savings deficiency at the target growth rate but it would not bolster inappropriate price policies and perpetuate misallocation of resources in the assisted economy.

On the other hand, if an economy genuinely faces 'structural' rigidities, no price or exchange rate policies will help to close the *ex-ante* gaps and foreign assistance flows should fill any larger 'trade' gap if the target growth is to be achieved. Foreign assistance may then be viewed as helping to weaken rigidities

a by financing the domestic development of a more diversified industrial structure capable of producing domestic substitutes for imports, and goods which have an elastic foreign demand; and

b by tiding over the period while developed countries alter their restrictive trade policies towards many developing country exports.

Let us now assume an economy with a genuine problem of inelastic exports and imports and an *ex-ante* gap inequality. How does the short-run adjustment from *ex-ante* inequality to *ex-post* equality come about?

In the first case where the 'hard core' *ex-ante* $M - X$ gap exceeds the *ex-ante* $I - S$ gap at the desired growth rate (r_1) *and* net foreign capital *actually* forthcoming fills the larger gap, there will be a deficiency of effective demand. This can be illustrated as follows: Suppose an economy is projected to have a net national income (Y) = 1000. Also that projected investment (I) = 200, savings (S) = 100, exports (X) = 100, imports (M) = 250. It is further assumed that foreign resources equivalent to the larger ($M - X$) gap are forthcoming (i.e. 150). Then aggregate demand for goods and services = $I + C = 200 + 900 = 1,100$ while supplies available for domestic use = $Y + M - X = 1000 + 250 - 100 = 1,150$. A deficiency of effective demand of 50 exists. If the general price level is inflexible downwards, market forces would cause unplanned stocks accumulation, reduced utilization of capacity and reduced impetus to invest.

This would mean a shortfall in the level of income and the target investment and growth rates. Even if prices are flexible there could be some loss of confidence by entrepreneurs with similar effects on investment and growth. The government will therefore have to intervene to stimulate domestic consumption (reduce domestic savings) by (say) reducing taxation to ensure that *ex-post* equality of the two gaps is realized without a change in desired investment and growth rate. It would be inappropriate to stimulate investment since this would conflict with the pre-determined growth target and also cause an unplanned increase in import requirements.

In the second case where the foreign resources forthcomings are equal to a dominant *ex-ante* $I - S$ gap at the target growth rate, there will be an excess of aggregate demand over aggregate supply at current prices. The appropriate government policy would be to stimulate the demand for imported consumer goods, or divert export goods which can be consumed at home, from foreign markets to the home market. This might be effected by changes in the exchange rate or in import duties and export taxes. To permit greater imports of capital goods might cause increased investment and hence widen the $I - S$ gap and foreign resources forthcoming would then be inadequate. In the absence of these policy measures there will be an accumulation of foreign exchange reserves and the domestic excess demand will cause unplanned stocks reduction or inflation. Even if fixed investment is unaffected, there will be an eventual replenishment of depleted stocks from imports (running down the increased foreign exchange reserves) or rising domestic prices will reduce exports, due to increased competition from domestic buyers and reduced foreign demand.

Hence, one way or another, the $M - X$ gap would adjust to the $I - S$ gap *ex post*. In the first case, however, it is important for the government to take the appropriate policy measures otherwise the adjustment may frustrate the target growth rate. In the second case, an absence of government intervention seems unlikely to affect target growth.

The preceding two chapters have considered the theoretical nature of the 'two gap' analysis of aid but it does not consider the usefulness of this approach to aid policy in practice. A sceptical view of the possibilities of this approach is provided in the last chapter of this book.

Notes

1   The most recent computations are those of UNCTAD, *Trade Prospects and Capital Needs of Developing Countries*, New York, 1968. A similar methodology has been used by A. Maizels *et al.*, *Exports and Economic Growth of Developing Countries*, N.I.E.S.R., 1968, to predict growth rates on certain assumptions about export growth of developing countries and plausible foreign capital inflows.

2   Net factor receipts and payments for the economy are assumed to be zero.

3   Note that in this model in Ch. 3, x represented the (constant) proportion of exports to income, whereas here x represents the growth in exports over time. The difference is that exports are exogenously determined and not set by growth of income.

4   Thus investment and saving are not a function of the rate of interest and exports and imports are not a function of the price of domestic relative to foreign traded goods and services.

5   It should be noted that even equality of the two gaps *ex ante* is not a sufficient condition of equilibrium (i.e. of achieving the specified growth targets) as in the Keynesian system. It also requires that *actual* foreign resources forthcoming are equal to the *ex-ante* gap.

6   The price of capital goods is assumed unchanged.

7   The most important manufactured consumer good exported from developing countries is cotton textiles and the global and country-wise quotas imposed on imports into developed economies, at present, give the foreign demand curve an effective kink which must frustrate any attempt to raise export earnings from price adjustments by the suppliers.

8   These are the basic Leontieff assumptions of fixed coefficients in production and consumption as opposed to the neo-classical assumptions of smooth continuous isoquants and preference/indifference curves.

9   India has been suggested as one country where a trade constraint or gap may well dominate the savings constraint or gap.

5

Debt and the terms of aid

Introduction

So far the analysis has been concerned with assessing the
effect of net capital inflows on growth, but no attention has
been given to the implications of indebtedness arising from
these capital flows and the servicing of the debt by the
borrowing country.

What effect will the need to service debt have on growth
of the borrower in the short run and long run?

The answer depends, of course, on the attitudes or policies
of the lending countries. Whether debt will present an
obstacle to desired growth rates of developing countries will
depend on the *scale* and the *terms* on which lenders are
prepared to transfer resources to these countries. This clearly
does not involve fundamental issues in growth theory.
Nevertheless from a policy viewpoint it is valuable to analyse
possible behaviour patterns of debt on different scales and
terms of capital inflow.

The debt-service issue will be analysed in the context of
long-run growth and also in the context of short-run
management. It will be assumed, that there is one lender and
one borrower. If the lender is only willing to lend for a
limited period on fixed terms (of interest and repayment)
then the long-run target growth rate in the borrowing
country will have to be tailored to allow a sufficient margin

of resources for servicing debt. If on the other hand, the lender is prepared to lend at interest in unlimited amounts for indefinite periods in order to permit the borrower to achieve a specified growth objective, there would appear to be no debt problem. Yet even in this case it can be shown that formally an 'unmanageable' debt problem can arise and cause a breakdown. Thus, if the interest rate on loans exceeds a certain 'critical' level, debt (and hence interest payments) may explode in relation to the gross national product of the borrower. The policy implication is that where growth conditions in the borrower seem unfavourable, interest rates must be kept below this critical level by the lender to ensure that no breakdown in the borrower's ability to meet interest charges occurs.

The debt problem is therefore essentially a problem of the terms on which assistance is provided. For the economic analyst the main interest lies in establishing the consistency of growth targets set by the borrower with the terms of capital assistance set by the lender. If lenders commit themselves to certain growth objectives in the borrowing country, the terms of assistance required to achieve these targets can be calculated formally using the type of simple macro-economic model employed in earlier chapters.

In addition to the long-run implications of debt servicing there is also the short-term problem. Against a background of fluctuating export earnings the borrowing economy is faced with rigid debt-service payments. This may present acute problems of short-run management especially if interest and amortization constitute a large proportion of export earnings.

These long-run and short-run issues will be discussed more fully in the following sections.

Debt and long-run growth

The economic conditions which must be fulfilled if the borrower is to service the debt arising can be stated formally

65

in terms of total resource availabilities and uses and foreign exchange availabilities and uses. These conditions are that:

1 output produced plus gross foreign capital inflow must exceed domestic consumption and investment by the amount of debt-service payments, *or* domestic savings plus capital inflow must exceed domestic investment by the amount of debt-service payments. And

2 foreign exchange receipts plus gross foreign capital inflow[1] must exceed payments for imports by the amount of the debt-service payments.

An economy must adjust claims on total resource, savings, and foreign exchange in any given year and over time so as to release the resources required to meet debt-service obligations. Formally there is nothing in the price or income adjustment mechanism which makes it impossible for this adjustment to be made if the rules of the game are kept. However, these adjustments may conflict with other central objectives of the debtor country; they may involve reduced employment and activity in the short run and lower investment levels and hence lower growth rates (than desired) in the long run.

Since the debt-servicing capacity of an economy is clearly related to its growth rate, it is most conveniently analysed in the context of a simple macro-economic model of the savings-investment kind employed earlier.

In this model the main parameters are average (s) and marginal ($\bar{s}$) savings rates, output capital ratio (δ) and the target growth rate of G.D.P. ($\bar{r}$). The required investment rate is then $\frac{\bar{r}}{\delta}$. For simplicity, though not realism, it is assumed that these parameters remain constant for the foreseeable future.

To build in the debt implications it is also necessary to assume a given average interest rate on foreign assistance (i). Now a borrowing economy can hypothetically pass through three stages in its debt profile and this is illustrated in Figure 5.

In *Stage one* domestic savings are inadequate to finance required investment and the economy has to borrow not only to finance part of the investment but also to pay interest on

Figure 5   Hypothetical debt profile

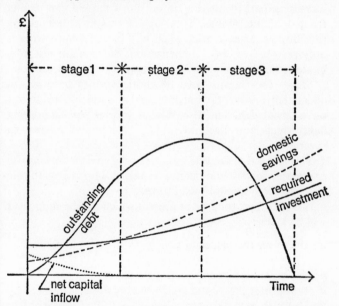

debt accumulated and to cover amortization. During this phase the burden of servicing foreign capital is continuously postponed and the debt compounds rapidly.

Stage two begins when domestic savings are adequate to finance required investment. The economy's target growth can now be potentially self-sustained. If the borrower decides not to default on debt-service payments it still has to borrow to pay these.[2]

F   67

This stage will only begin (in terms of this model) if the marginal savings rate ($\bar{s}$) is at least equal to the required investment rate, since in the long run the average domestic savings rate will tend towards the marginal rate. During this stage no *net* inflow of capital is required but new borrowing continues to finance interest and repayment of borrowed capital. As average domestic savings continue to grow an increasing part of interest on outstanding debt can be met from domestic savings. Total debt grows at a diminishing rate till it reaches a peak when new external borrowing is only required to cover amortization. Savings are just adequate to finance required investment and interest on debt.

Stage three begins when domestic savings have grown adequately to cover not only required investment and interest on external debt but also yield a surplus for amortizing debt which now declines rapidly (compound interest in reverse).

This stylized debt cycle indicates how an economy can be assisted to achieve and maintain a self-sustained growth rate and still repay capital with interest.

It is clear that the rate of growth which can be supported will be lower:

a   the lower the marginal savings ratio ($\bar{s}$)
b   the lower the output/capital ratio (δ)
c   the higher the interest rate on loans (i)
d   the shorter the period which the borrower is allowed by the lender to become independent of capital assistance or free of debt.

However, there is nothing automatic or inevitable about this growth process and debt cycle. The growth process is not as mechanical and predictable as this simple model assumes.

There are some economies which, on present evidence, seem unlikely to leave stage one. These are the economies where low marginal savings rates suggest that domestic saving in the foreseeable future will not cover their investment requirement for sustaining a 'satisfactory' growth rate. These 'long haul' countries will tend to be those with large population relative to natural resources, low *per capita* income and high population growth rates. Such economies could remain borrowers indefinitely and could only sustain their target growth rates if the lender is prepared to lend indefinitely.

There are other economies which are likely to become *just* self-sustaining in growth, (i.e. enter stage two where domestic savings equal required investment). Interest payments will then increase annually at a rate equal to the rate of interest. Once again the country would have to borrow indefinitely whatever the interest rate (if it is other than zero). For economies which become *more than* just self-sustaining, the behaviour of debt and the borrowing horizon will depend on the level of interest rates charged.

Indefinite borrowing and the critical interest rate

The maintenance of desired growth rates in certain economies will depend, therefore, on the willingness of the lender to lend indefinitely. There is no *a priori* answer to whether these conditions will be met. However, if unlimited borrowing is possible, it is important to note that 'unmanageable' debt can still arise for the borrower if debt (and hence interest payments) rise faster than its national product. Unlimited borrowing and debt rising for ever is manageable provided it does not 'explode' relative to national income. There is a 'critical' rate of interest on borrowed funds above which this explosion will occur; and this can be demonstrated as follows:

In the long run the average saving rate (s) will approach more and more closely to the marginal savings rate ($\bar{s}$). Thus the surplus of domestic savings over required investment, needed to service debt, will approach the proportion of G.N.P. equal to the difference between marginal savings and required investment. At one extreme, when the surplus just covers interest obligations debt is constant. At the other extreme when there is no surplus, debt grows at a rate equal to the rate of interest (i). If this rate of interest exceeds the growth of G.N.P. then debt ultimately becomes unmanageable.

In between these two long-run extremes lies the critical case where debt would grow at the *same* rate as national product. It is possible to identify a 'critical interest rate' which is a function of initial and marginal savings rates, the output–capital ratio and desired growth rate.[3]

The policy implication is clear for the lender. In certain cases it may not only be necessary to lend indefinitely to sustain desired growth rates but it may also be necessary to adjust the interest rate on loans to ensure that debt does not explode relative to the G.N.P. of the borrower.

Whether the concept of the critical interest rate is significant is more debatable. If a country is unlikely to become self-sustaining in growth and must borrow indefinitely, it seems pointless to charge interest at all. Charging a positive interest rate only goes to swell an unrepayable debt indefinitely.[4]

If, on the other hand, a country can become more than self-sustaining (so that the critical interest is higher than the rate of growth) then it is hardly vital to calculate the critical interest rate since in this situation the borrower can default on his debt-service obligation without jeopardizing his desired growth rate.

In any case, these calculations are excessively formal and, in practice, it is not interest rates so much as the willingness of lenders to continue providing resources to the borrowers which is likely to be the obstacle to sustaining necessary growth rates in the long run. There are also short-term management problems arising for the borrower in meeting debt-service obligations.

Short-run debt servicing

Interest on debt is the most rigid item in a country's balance of payments and must normally be paid in convertible currency. Export earnings, the main source of convertible currency, however, are often subject to considerable fluctuations in borrowing countries.[5] As interest payments rise to a large proportion of a borrower's export earnings, the rigidity becomes of greater significance.

In principle, there is no problem if the lenders provide adequate new loans to cover necessary imports as well as the debt-service obligations. In practice, however, liquidity problems can arise if the new loans are inconvertible (e.g. tied to the purchase of goods in the lending country). Capital inflows of this kind are not perfectly substitutable for debt-service payments made in convertible currency.

In the later stage of the debt cycle when the debtor country has become a net repayer of capital there is still no formal problem. When exports fall a deflation of domestic income will reduce imports until a sufficient margin of foreign exchange is released to pay the fixed debt-service charges. In practice, however, the structure of the economy may make it so difficult to substitute domestically for many imports (especially fuel, industrial maintenance goods and certain capital goods) that drastic reductions in the utilization of existing capacity and the level or the productivity of the domestic investment programme may be necessary to ensure that foreign exchange uses and availabilities are balanced.

An escape from this problem may be found in the use of foreign exchange reserves and stabilization policies by the exporting country but again experience suggests that many difficulties can arise. The management of many developing countries' balance of payments may be considerably complicated therefore by the need to service debt. Where management is inefficient, long-run growth can be reduced.

71

Notes

1 Including any net call on the borrower's foreign exchange reserves.

2 Clearly this is the point at which a single borrower can default with no cost and much saving to itself. From a purely economic viewpoint the main discouragement to it defaulting lies in the possibility that its own growth parameters will change unfavourably in future or that its behaviour will dry up the supply of capital to other developing countries who have not yet reached the stage of potentially self-sustained growth.

3 The concept of the critical interest rate is due to J. P. Hayes. The critical interest rate (i) is given by the following formula when initial period debt is zero and S_0 represents the savings rate in the initial period.

$$I = \frac{r(S_0 - \bar{s})}{S_0 - \dfrac{r}{\delta}}$$

It is noticeable that even if the marginal savings rate ($\bar{s}$) is less than the desired investment rate a country can borrow indefinitely without interest payments continuously increasing faster than domestic product, provided interest rates are low enough (obviously if $i = 0$).

4 However lending governments may in practice be under two forms of pressure which require them to lend indefinitely but at positive interest rates. On the one hand, there is the moral and political pressure to assist very poor countries indefinitely. On the other hand there is the influence of an ethical system which insists on the obligation of the borrower to repay with interest. This is further supported by the contention that unless interest is charged the borrower will use the funds inefficiently. (There is no *a priori* or (yet) empirical justification for this view however.)

5 Unstable export earnings are said to arise in primary producing countries because they are often dependent on a narrow range of export commodities whose markets are affected by minor recessions in industrial countries and whose supply is often vulnerable to bad harvests, domestic political instability, etc. The rigidity of debt payments has also increased in recent years as developing countries have come to rely more heavily on borrowing from other governments. Previously most of the capital inflow was in the form of private equity invested in export industries. This ensured that profit and dividend remittances fluctuated with fluctuations in export earnings.

6

Aid tying: trade
and resource allocation effects

What is tying?

External financial assistance to developing countries is provided in a wide variety of forms. This is largely a matter of the degree of restriction placed by the provider of the finance on the *use* to which these resources should be put and the *sources* from which they should be obtained. At one extreme is completely untied finance which the recipient can use for any purpose and which can be used to procure goods and services from any international source. At the other extremes would be finance tied to procurement of goods in the assisting country and tied to use on a specific project (or for specific goods) in the recipient country. There are a variety of intermediate forms. In practice the forms of aid will vary greatly for different countries but there has been a general trend towards increased 'source-tying' of aid since 1960.

There are two main economic reasons why aid is tied by source and use:

First, aiding countries are concerned with the effect which aid has on their exports. This concern with the trade effects of aid arises because an important 'lobby' supporting development assistance in developed countries are certain domestic industries which hope to profit from export contracts under this assistance. Further, the governments of aiding countries are often concerned about the cost of aid to their own balance of payments. They wish to minimize the charge which their aid programmes make on their foreign exchange reserves especially if their reserves are inadequate.[1]

Second, the 'aiding country wishes to' exert influence over the allocation of resources in the recipient. Whether tying makes this feasible has been the subject of some debate among economists. Suppose, for example, that aid is tied to project A which is examined and considered 'high priority' by the aiding country. If this project would, in any case, have been part of the recipient country's investment programme and would otherwise have been undertaken with the country's own resources, then the project *actually* financed would be quite another one from that to which the aid is ostensibly tied. Tying can be effective in this respect if the aiding and the aided countries differ in their assessment of investment priorities, but this raises the important question of which country is the best judge of development priorities.[2]

The rest of this chapter is devoted to a simple analysis of the effects of aid tying on (*a*) Trade Patterns and (*b*) Resource Allocation.

Aid tying and trade patterns

To examine the effect of aid tying on trade patterns a simple arithmetical example is used with one recipient country importing from three other countries, two of which provide aid. It is assumed that any aid provided will in *aggregate* generate an equivalent quantity of extra imports, i.e. that a typical developing country is assumed not to add to its reserves when it receives aid in any period. The analysis will consider the trade effects of a marginal addition to aid.

a   *Untied aid*

When aid is completely untied it can be used for any item from any source. Since Recipient can purchase aided imports from its most preferred sources, the import pattern on untied aid will be the 'free trade' pattern. In the following example, therefore, recipient's average propensity to import from different sources out of its own earned foreign exchange is taken to represent the 'free trade' pattern of its imports. These average propensities are assumed to operate when untied aid is spent.[3] In this situation it is highly unlikely that aid provided by each *individual* country will generate an equivalent amount of its own export to Recipient. This will only occur if recipient's free trade (f.t.) propensity to import from each aiding country is the same as each donor's share of a marginal increment of aid to recipient. Such an occurrence would be purely coincidental since the f.t. propensities to import from different countries will depend on its commodity pattern of imports and the comparative advantage of the various countries supplying these commodities, while the share of each country in aid to Recipient will depend on various factors which are not likely to be systematically related trade shares.[4]

Table 8 provides a simple illustration of the untied aid/ trade situation.

Table 8   Recipient's imports with untied aid

	Imports without aid	Untied aid	Aided imports	Total imports
Country A	400 (40%)	60	40	440 (40%)
B	500 (50%)	40	50	550 (50%)
C	100 (10%)	—	10	110 (10%)
	1000	100	100	1100

The provision of untied aid leaves the overall import pattern (by source) unchanged. However, aiding country A gains only 40 extra imports for 60 untied aid, while countries B and C gain more exports than their aid contributions.

b Unilateral tying

If A has a balance of payments problem it will be under pressure to tie its aid to raise its export/aid ratio. Let us consider now the trade effects of unilateral tying by A, i.e., on the assumption that other donors do not respond by tying themselves. The trade effects of tying by A will depend on its form of tying. We can distinguish conceptually two cases of tying and their effectiveness in altering trade patterns.

Case 1 Tying to source only If country A ties its aid to procurement of commodities only from A but leaves the recipient free choice of commodities, such tying may be completely ineffective in generating extra exports. This will certainly be the case if the tied aid is used to purchase goods which would have been bought from A anyway, and the total value of the goods which would be bought from A without aid exceeds the amount of A's aid. A's aid is then said to be 'switched' and the trade/aid relationship between A and the recipient will be exactly the same as in the untied aid situation. In the Table 8 example A's source tied aid of 60 is 'switched' and releases Recipient's own free exchange resources for spending according to its free trade propensity to import from the three countries, A, B and C. A gains no more exports from 'source-tying' its aid; such tying is purely formal and has no trade diversionary effects.

Case 2 Tying to source and use Suppose A not only confines expenditure from its aid to A's goods but also specifies the *use* of the aid. Two sub-cases can be distinguished where such double-tying will be effective in diverting trade to A.

The first case is where aid is tied to a *marginal* project—

a project which Recipient would not otherwise have under-taken.[5] Aid is then used for the purchase of imports from A which would not otherwise have been made from any source.

In this way A alters the pattern of Recipient's trade in its favour and it will be seen from the illustrative example in Table 9 that A not only ensures that its own aid is 100% effective in generating extra exports but also it gains some exports at the expense of other donors (still untied) aid.

The second case is where A's aid is in *non-project* form, but tied to goods which the recipient would otherwise import from the other countries B and C. This type of tying is deliberately aggressive and aimed at diverting Recipient's imports from its most preferred sources. This type of tying is harmful to the recipient since it forces it to import from sources which do not necessarily have a comparative advantage in the commodities concerned. This reduces the value of aid provided; a problem that will be taken up in the next section.

Table 9   *Recipient's imports – A's aid tied to marginal project*

Country	Imports without aid	Aid	Imports from tied aid	Imports* from untied aid	Total imports
A	400 (40%)	60	60	16	476 (43·6%)
B	500 (50%)	40	—	20	520 (47·3%)
C	100 (10%)	—	—	4	104 (9·1%)
	1000	100			1100

* i.e. Total untied aid (40) × propensity to import from each country.

Our concern here is to show that trade is diverted from the most preferred sources by this type of tying. The situation is illustrated in Table 10. It will be seen that A's aid is used to

77

buy goods which would otherwise have been bought from B and C, and hence releases Recipient's own foreign exchange resources to use freely according to its free trade propensity to import from different sources. The net effect is to shift the trade pattern even more in A's favour than aid which is untied or tied to a marginal project.[6]

Table 10   Recipient's imports – with tied non-project aid

Country	Imports without aid	Aid	Import diversion through tied aid	Imports from freely usable resources (c)	Total imports
A	400	60 (a)	+60	+40	500 (45·5%)
B	500	40 (b)	−50	+50	500 (45·5%)
C	100		−10	+10	100 (9·0%)
	1000				1100

(a) tied, (b) untied, (c) i.e. untied aid + free resources released by A's tied aid.

c   *Reciprocal tying*

This deliberate diversion of trade through A's tying practice is likely to spark off a 'tying war', with other donors reciprocating these tying practices to regain some of their lost trade. In this simple model the only other aiding country B would now tie its aid to goods which would otherwise have been supplied by A or C. In this situation it is impossible to say *a priori* how the final trade pattern will be distorted from that where all aid is untied. This will depend on the country-wise incidence of the trade diversion, effects of each donors tied aid and the shares of aid provided. It should be noted that aid tying of this kind can displace the trade of other poor countries with Recipient.

Many poor countries are faced with difficulty in expanding their exports to the markets of the developed countries. Greater intra-trade between developing countries would help to circumvent this problem. In so far as aid tying limits trade between poor countries it is working against one of the main purposes for which aid is provided – i.e. to relieve a foreign exchange constraint in the developing country.

So far we have been concerned with the effects of aid tying on trade patterns. This is the main concern of the donors. However, the greater the degree of tying imposed by countries in protecting their uncompetitive export industries or their balance of payments position, the more is the value of a given amount of aid reduced to the recipient.[7] This issue will now be examined.

Aid tying – effects on recipient countries

Aid tying generally reduces the value of a given amount of aid to the recipient country. Because aid is tied by source, and often to specific commodities, the recipient is not able to purchase goods from those sources which have a comparative advantage in producing them. Aid tying, therefore, may force recipients into non-optimal patterns of resource allocation (which are not the result of their own inefficient domestic policies). This problem can be analysed and illustrated formally by some fairly simple models.

Model I Source-tied aid

Let us assume, initially, that Recipient produces a single product and no exports. No domestic factors are required for production but two inputs, A and B, are imported on aid which is tied to purchases in the two aid-giving countries I and II. Source-tied aid is therefore the only way of financing the required inputs. It is assumed that the supply of input A is cheapest from source I and input B is cheapest from source II; prices being fixed at the source of supply. Finally the production function in Recipient is assumed to have isoquants convex to the origin. In Figure 6, A_1B_1 represents the available combinations of A and B under aid from source I where A is cheaper. A_2B_2 is the equivalent aid availability line from source II where B is cheaper. The total tied aid

Figure 6 Aid tying

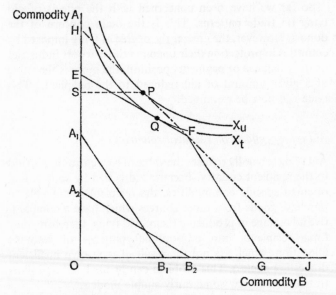

vailability line is EFG (Where $FG \parallel$ to A_1B_1 and $EF \parallel$ to A_2B_2 and $OE = OA_1 + OA_2$ and $OG = OB_1 + OB_2$).

If the same total aid were *untied* to source, the aid availability line would be HFJ[8] which represents all possible combinations of A and B bought at their cheapest source. It is only at combination F that the two inputs can be bought at their cheapest source when aid is tied, and it is only by coincidence that the highest isoquant would touch EFG

(tied aid availability curve) at F. It is likely to touch at some point such as Q on isoquant X_t. At Q, output is sub-optimal in relation to the level possible with untied aid, (point P on isoquant X_u). The domestic price ratio for the two inputs (= marginal rate of substitution between them) at equilibrium Q, would diverge from the 'best' international price ratio (the slope of HJ).

Aid tying in this case not only distorts the allocation of resources in the recipient country, it can have the same effect on the donor country. In the above case not all requirements of input A can be met from the cheapest source (I). Hence there is a demand in source II on the industry producing A which has a comparative cost disadvantage relative to B.

Model II Source and commodity-tied aid
If aid is tied to commodities as well as source in a very rigid way, then resource allocation is again made non-optimal in the recipient country. For example, suppose source I will provide a fixed quantity OA_2 of good A only and source II will provide OB of good B only on aid. The amount of output produced with these inputs would lie on the isoquant passing through F. If HJ represents the international price ratio for A and B, then F is a sub-optimal position, where the domestic price ratio diverges from the international price ratio.

If aid were tied rigidly to source and commodity in this way F would be on an even lower isoquant (or level of output) than if aid were merely source tied (i.e. Q).[9]

This may be a somewhat extreme case which arises where aid is provided in kind (e.g. wheat or cotton surpluses under U.S. P.L. 480 aid). However if aid is tied to the purchase of a limited range of goods (quantities not rigidly specified) as well as source, the analysis under Model I does not reveal explicitly a further reason why tying reduces the value of aid to the recipient. This is the opportunity which 'source and item' tying provides for 'monopolistic' pricing by industries in the donor countries.

It will be remembered that Model I assumed that the prices of A and B were set at the source of supply. These prices, however, need not be 'competitive' prices. If, as happens frequently in practice, donor governments specify both source *and items* permitted under their aid, then the specific donor industry producing these goods becomes, in effect, the only source of supply. When the suppliers of these items are few in number 'collusion' in fixing prices above the competitive level can occur on aid contracts.[10] Even if collusion does not take place the recipient of aid is likely to suffer from monopolistic 'price discrimination'.

It is well known in formal economic theory that a monopolistic supplier will maximize his profits by charging a higher price in his domestic market and a lower price in the international market where the demand curve is normally more elastic. If the supplying firms in the donor country treat aid-financed sales as equivalent to *domestic* sales they will charge the higher monopolistic price rather than their competitive export price for the same commodity.[11] This means that double-tied aid is worth less in real terms to the recipient than equivalent untied aid which can be used to buy any items from any international source. Moreover, even if the source to which the aid is tied has a comparative cost advantage in a particular commodity (e.g. A from source I) the recipient may not fully benefit from this. Formally, in terms of Figure 1, double-tying resulting in 'collusion' and/or 'price discrimination' practices at source, will shift the aid availability curve EFG to the left (compared with a situation where competitive prices for A and B are charged at the supply source). In this model the recipients will now operate on a lower isoquant than X_t.

The above model is unrealistic in assuming that the recipient country produces only one product which is not exported and which is produced with only imported resources. If these assumptions are relaxed it can be shown that the recipient of tied aid can mitigate the adverse effects of tying on the available level of real resources and their optimum allocation.

Substitution possibilities

Recipient can effectively untie aid, which is formally tied to source, if, from its own export earnings, it would have purchased anyway some goods from the aid sources. The conditions are that (*a*) aid is tied to source only, (*b*) the value of the tied aid does not exceed the value of the goods it would have purchased in any case from a given source, (*c*) the aid-giving source does not insist that aid purchases should be 'additional' to purchases which would have been made anyway.[12]

If a recipient can fully exploit these substitution possibilities, even though aid is tied, it can avoid non-optimal allocation of resources. Thus, suppose in the case above, Recipient would have liked to buy OB_3 of goods B from source II from non-aid funds.[13] It would also buy SP of B from source I on tied aid anyway because P is an optimal point. If $OB_3 + SP$ exceeds the amount of tied aid available from source II (OB_2) this aid is effectively untied. Total aid is also effectively untied since all the aid from source I would be used to purchase A from this source under optimal conditions. Hence Recipient by switching its tied aid from source I to finance purchases which would otherwise have been made from this source, releases free exchange to buy goods A from its cheapest source. The aid availability line then effectively becomes HJ.

Model III   A more realistic model

A more realistic model can be constructed by assuming that Recipient, uses domestic resources for production, produces more than one good and exports goods which finance the import of goods in addition to those available on aid. It is also assumed that the donor country insists on and achieves 'additionality' so that Recipient cannot substitute tied aid for financing imports it would otherwise have made from its export earnings.

Figure 7   Aid tying

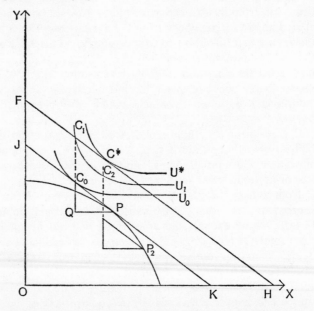

This situation is illustrated in Figure 7. Recipient can produce two commodities X and Y with domestic resources and the production possibility curve is convex. If JK is the international price ratio the country would produce a combination P. With the social welfare function represented by the U curves, the country would consume combination C_0 (exporting QP of X and importing QC_0 of Y). A single donor provides aid equivalent to KH of X or FJ of Y goods if aid were untied. However, the donor demands 'additionality' by

84

specifying that the recipient should import GH of Y (on aid) in addition to its import QC of Y from its own resources.

The optimal consumption would be C^* with untied aid. With the aid tied to Y and 'additional', one *possible* equilibrium would be C_1. This is clearly suboptimal and would require a consumption tax/subsidy policy.

A 'second-best' optimization policy permitting a higher level of welfare than C_1 could be achieved by an appropriate tax-cum-subsidy policy permitting the use of all the aid but changing the domestic output pattern in favour of X from P to P_2. This might yield a position C_2 which is preferable to C_1 but still a lower level of welfare than C^* under untied aid.

Empirical aspects

The preceding analysis assumes that in the aid-receiving country there is full knowledge of production functions and unambiguous social welfare functions so that optimum positions would be taken if the tying practices of aiding countries did not prevent this. This, of course, is not always the view of the government providing the aid. One of their reasons for tying is implicitly that they consider themselves a better judge of priorities in the allocation of resources than the local planners. This seems to imply either that their technical (production) knowledge is superior and/or that their relative valuation of different goods more nearly reflects the valuation of the aid-receiving society than that of the society's politicians and planners. This important issue cannot be discussed any further here but to some extent it requires an empirical answer.

Is there any empirical evidence on the magnitude of aid-tying inefficiencies? Clearly the extent to which tying interferes with the optimum choice of investment projects and techniques in the recipient country is largely unquantifiable. However, some qualification of the direct cost of aid tying (by source) is possible. The direct cost of aid tying can be defined for empirical purposes as the excess of the delivered price actually paid for goods by the recipient over the lowest delivered price which the country would have to pay if aid were not tied. The practical difficulties of measurement stem from lack of comparability of products imported from different sources and the problem of obtaining information on comparative prices from international tenders. Such evidence as exists[1] on Pakistan, Chile, Iran and Tunisia suggests that tying raises the procurement price of goods at least 10–20% above the price from the cheapest alternative source of supply.

Notes

1 This would suggest that those donors with the greatest 'liquidity' problems would be the ones which tie their aid most strictly. Observation, however, does not confirm this correlation.
2 See H. Singer, 'External Aid: For Plans or Projects', *Economic Journal*, September 1965.
3 In other words, the marginal propensity to import from different sources is assumed to be the same as the average. This may be unrealistic as the composition of imports will change as more resources become available for import. However, the assumption is used for simplicity.
4 There may be some relationship because historical ties between countries affect their trade and aid relationships (e.g., U.K. and certain Commonwealth countries; U.S. and Latin America). See Ch. 1 above.
5 It is impossible to ascertain by direct observation whether a project is marginal since it involves a comparison of an actual situation (with aid) and the hypothetical situation (without aid). Some inference may be made in practice, however.
6 The precise diversionary effects of A's tied aid on other individual countries cannot be specified *a priori*. It is assumed in Table 10 that they occur in proportion to the free trade shares of B and C in Recipient's imports. It is clear, however, that A gains at the expense of other exporters *as a whole* by this type of tying. The size of the trade gain will depend on the free trade propensities to import and Recipient's non-aided imports relative to aid.
7 It also does long-run damage to the export trade of the aiding country.

8   $HFJ \parallel A_1B_2$.

9   If the aid sources tied their aid to that commodity in which they had a comparative cost disadvantage (A from source II and B from source I) the recipient would find that its loss of output from aid tying would be greater still.

10   It may be possible for the aid-giving authority to examine prices and prevent this practice. Administratively, this often presents great difficulty because of the range of goods, the comparability problem and the detailed knowledge of prices required.

11   This may not occur systematically since not all firms follow such pricing practices. However, there is empirical evidence that generally domestic prices and f.o.b. (competitive) prices differ in industrial countries.

12   When no imports from a source would otherwise have been made, there is no scope for substitution. However, condition (c) is difficult to enforce in practice, since it is not possible to infer the amount of goods which would hypothetically have been purchased in the absence of aid. In practice, a donor may be very effective in achieving 'additionality' if it specifies items purchasable under tied aid which the recipient has been observed not to purchase in the past from it out of its own foreign exchanges. A policy of this kind, however, would seem to defeat the whole objective of aid by tying it to goods which have a low or zero development value.

13   For some other use than the production of X in the above simple model.

14   See bibliography.

7

Some questions and further issues

The preceding chapters have been concerned with setting up
an analytical framework for the economics of aid. If these
chapters have succeeded in giving the reader a simple,
orderly conceptual apparatus for approaching aid issues they
will have fulfilled their intention. But the simplicity and
neatness of the analysis is misleading and dangerous because
the development process and the role of aid is infinitely
more complex and subtle than these simple models and
principles suggest. It is salutary to end on a somewhat
sceptical note in case the impression is given that economists
know more than they really do about the key factors in
economic growth or that the preceding analysis provides
any more than a first step in providing a basis for aid policy
decisions.

This chapter will briefly raise a number of questions about
(*a*) The role of capital in economic growth, (*b*) the use of
performance criteria for allocation of aid, (*c*) the use of
aggregate models for aid policy, (*d*) the relationship of trade
and aid policy in development.

Role of capital and other factors in growth

With little qualification the underlying rationale of aid has
been that capital formation is an essential and major factor

in growth and traditionally much economic theory has provided support for this view. Foreign capital is typically seen as a supplement to domestic savings which enables domestic investment to be higher than it would be on the basis of domestic efforts alone. A predictable, and often fixed, relationship is postulated between investment during a period and the extra flow of output, assumed to be generated by it.

This view which relates output growth to a single factor – capital invested in physical goods – strains credulity. It takes little perception to realize that many other factors than financially measured investment must determine any extra measured output which is produced in a period. The importance of the appropriate skills of the labour force, the enterprise and organizational capacity of those making decisions, the natural environment and the timing of discoveries of new natural resources, the level of technical knowledge and the stability of the political environment are only some of the other general influences on economical productive activity.

Casual observation reveals that some countries have had rapid growth without significant capital formation and without substantial capital import; others have had high rates of investment and external assistance yet low growth rates. Neither extra domestic capital formation nor more external capital is a necessary or sufficient condition for faster growth.

Recent systematic analysis, which cannot directly answer questions of causality, has nevertheless suggested that investment rates in different economies 'explain' only a small part of the observed differences in the growth rates of these economies. Other factors appear much more important and these may not be universal factors but influences which are specific to each economy.

In any case, is it the savings and investment which generate the growth or is it the growth which generates the opportunities for productive investment and the conditions for high

89

savings propensities? There is clearly a two-way relationship which raises even more doubts about the interpretation of the observed statistical association between investment and domestic savings rates, on one hand, and growth rates on the other.

The answer to these fundamental growth questions is highly relevant to any theory of aid or aid policy. Can we say only that in environments where conditions are favourable to growth, capital inflows will be highly effective and that where aid is likely to fall on stony ground it should not be made available? Or can aid be used directly or indirectly to *create* more favourable growth conditions? Can externally financed and chosen projects break bottlenecks in an economy and so create growth conditions or stimulate new economic activities by their demonstration effects? Or are foreign financed projects more likely to do harm than good? It has been contended, for example, that aid-financed projects are frequently too grandiose, too capital or import intensive and too unrelated to the requirements of the domestic economy. Aiding governments or their officials may, for various reasons, have a bias towards financing large industrial or overhead projects. This may cause a diversion of local resources and interest from smaller projects in the agricultural sector of developing economies which might well yield higher returns and relieve a major constraint on growth.

More indirectly, should aid be used as a 'carrot and stick' device to induce governments of certain developing countries to follow policies and activities likely to be more favourable to growth and development? This raises the question of 'performance criteria' in aid allocation, which is discussed at greater length below.

Performance criteria

The suggestion has frequently been made that aid should be made dependent or conditional on the performance of the recipient. The idea has considerable appeal to those who think help should be given to those who help themselves. In Chapter 2 one such criterion discussed was the proposal to make aid available only to those countries likely to become independent of aid in a given period of time. Several major problems arise in this type of approach. First, what are the development objectives against which judgment is to be made? Growth of conventionally measured national product (or national product per head)? This largely ignores other elements which might be termed 'quality of life' factors as well as the distribution of measurable income. It is possible of course to devise 'composite' indicators of development which bring together quantitative indices of its various strands such as indices of improvement in the educational system, health and nutrition and measures of political and social stability where they can be devised. However, apart from the problem of choosing the relevant components, what weight is to be given to them in the sum? Difficult value judgments are involved here but does the composite index present any greater problem than that involved in using national product indices which weight the components by their market valuation?

An alternative approach is to measure a country's performance by 'intermediate' variables considered to be instrumental in development; such as savings rates, export growth, tax revenue. Whatever variables are used a further problem arises – the need to distinguish between performance and success; between the controllable and the uncontrollable elements in an economy's observed growth, savings, exports or any other target variables.

Ideally, aid should be related to that part of the observed outcome which is under the control of the government of a country. Because too little is known about the precise impact of various policy measures it is not possible in practice to identify the controllable elements in the situation. An improvement in the savings rate of a country may be due

91

to greater tax efforts or to a fortuitous change in the terms of trade.

A third problem arises, even if performance can be measured in a meaningful way. This is the weight to be attached to 'poverty' as distinct from 'performance' in the allocation of assistance. This presents very difficult value judgments for the aiding countries since the poorest countries are often likely to be the worst performers.

Aggregate models

Whether 'performance' tests are used or not there is a need to estimate the volume as well as the nature of external capital flows required by developing countries. There are, in brief, two approaches to the problem – macro and the micro methods. Aggregate growth models which provide a method for estimating the aggregate resource gap have been discussed at some length in Chapters 3 and 4. Attention must now be drawn to the weakness of this approach in practice and the alternative (or at least supplementary) view of total aid inflows as the sum of a series of micro-economic analyses and decisions.

The aggregate two-gap models examined in earlier chapters have many attractions. To the tidy-minded theorist they are neat, clear-cut and rigorous. The growth process is reduced to a simple mechanical model whose parameters can be altered to see what the implications are for aid flows. To the policy maker these models are also attractive. They provide an objective (a target rate of self-sustained growth), some performance standards in the aided country (e.g. domestic savings rates or export growth rates) and a method of calculating the volume and duration of aid flows required to achieve the objective.

Theoretical questions about these macro-models have already been raised in earlier chapters. Here it is necessary to consider the weaknesses of these models as a practical guide to policy.

In the first place the models are too mechanical. They can only be relied on to predict future aid requirements if it can be assumed that the values of the parameters will remain stable in future or that past experience is an accurate guide to future behaviour. This is often highly implausible. In the early stages of development, for example, heavy investment in infrastructure may be necessary to establish conditions for future growth and the capital–output ratio which prevailed at this stage would be valueless as a guide to that likely at later stages of development. Similarly, marginal savings rates can shift radically over time – both upwards and downwards depending on domestic conditions and policies. In practice, therefore, no long-run predictions could be safely made from these models and continuous assessment would be necessary; based on informed judgment about the behaviour of the main parameters and not merely on statistical projection.

In the second place, the aggregate nature of these models makes no allowance for the absorptive capacity of the economy for capital. The ability of a country to formulate and execute productive projects is not taken directly into account in aggregate exercises of this nature. Local skills, administrative capacities and experience may effectively constrain the amount of capital inflow that can be productively used in a given period below the amount that aggregate models may suggest. The result would be a diversion of some or all of the capital inflow into consumption.

Thirdly, aggregate models do not indicate the appropriate allocation of aid. Where are the bottlenecks? Where is the rate of return highest? These are micro-economic questions which involve a detailed examination of the different sectors, industries and projects and require techniques of cost-benefit appraisal and linear programming. They require much data collection, enquiry and local judgment over a wide area. This approach to aid requirements is less spectacular and simple but is likely to come much closer to assessing the

93

appropriate aid flows for a particular country as well as the most strategic points to which it should flow.

Since one of aid's vital functions is to relieve strategic shortages and bottlenecks in various sectors or areas of an economy, it cannot be viewed simply as an aggregate supplement to domestic resources. Its importance lies largely in its disaggregate nature and impact at many different points and places.

The appraisal of projects considered for foreign capital assistance, involves the study of investment economics and cost-benefit analysis. An introduction to this field is provided in a companion book in this series (*Investment Economics* by J. L. Carr).[1] It is hardly necessary to add that to make an effective appraisal of projects at the micro-level, it is necessary to have knowledge of the prospective total or macro-situation in an economy. To this extent both micro and macro analysis are complementary to one another in the difficult task of assessing the scale, pattern and impact of aid flows.

Aid and trade

Discussion in this book has been confined to the economics of aid and nothing has been said about the trade policies of the wealthier countries and their effect on developing countries.

What is the relationship between trade and aid? Are they substitutes or complements?

Some trade measures designed to help the export earnings of developing countries involve an implicit transfer of resources and therefore have a certain aid content. International Commodity Agreements to raise primary product prices or preferential trading arrangements that permit less developed countries to charge higher prices for their industrial products in developed country markets, involve an explicit resource transfer. This is a direct transfer from the consumers in developed countries to the governments or individuals of less developed countries.

Most trade measures (such as reduced tariffs or quantitative restrictions) taken by developed countries would increase export opportunities to developing countries. They involve no direct resource transfer. However, is there a sense in which increased trading opportunities are substitutable for aid?

It has been argued, for example, that aid is a 'soft option'. For the rich countries it is easier politically to place the burden of assisting development on the taxpayer (via aid) than to overcome the resistance of domestic producers to commercial policies which would expose them to greater competition from producers in the developing countries (e.g. textiles). For the poor countries, moreover, the artificial barriers to their exports in developed countries may force them to establish domestic industries which replace imports. These industries are often inefficient because they are sheltered by protection from the need to compete internationally. Inefficiency can therefore be encouraged in both rich and poor countries because it *seems* easier to provide aid than to provide freer access to developed country markets. Aid, in fact, may be financing some of the unsuitable, uncompetitive import-saving industries which developing countries are partly forced to establish because the industries where they have a comparative advantage over the rich countries (textiles, leather goods, etc.) are restricted in access to the rich country markets.

It is possible to show (following Professor H. Johnson) that greater trade opportunities may be compared to greater aid flows.

Clearly additional trade opportunities do not provide additional real resources for investment like aid. Instead, they provide the opportunity to convert extra domestic resources into foreign resources without the costs that would result if the trade opportunities did not exist. If the alternative were to establish import-saving industries, the cost of this is the extent to which domestic production of import-substitutes exceeds their world price. If the alternative were to sell more exports by lowering prices then the cost is the difference between the price at which they would be sold given the trade opportunity and the marginal revenue from selling more exports without the opportunity. In both cases the opportunity cost of the extra trade opportunity represents a real resource gain (like aid) to the country receiving it. These are the gains of maximum specialization.

Although greater trade possibilities for developing countries have some resource transfer element in them, they clearly are more *complementary* to aid flows than substitutable for them. Development requires both; the greatest scope for specialization and trade as well as external resources for investment to exploit these opportunities to the fullest possible extent.

Notes

1   An excellent practical guide to industrial investment appraisal in the context of developing countries is *Manual of Industrial Project Analysis*, Vol. II, by I. M. D. Little and J. A. Mirrlees, O.E.C.D., 1969.

Appendix

Resource gap models: statistical estimation of the parameters

The *ex-ante* and *ex-post* relationship between growth and foreign capital inflows were examined in the context of an aggregate model in Chapter 4. The three major structural parameters in the model were:

(i) The marginal output–investment relation (and) or its universe the incremental capital–output ratio (I.C.O.R.)
(ii) The savings–income relation: the marginal savings ratio ($\bar{s}$)
(iii) The relationship of imports to income: the marginal propensity to import ($\bar{m}$).

The behaviour of exports can also be related to income in the same way as imports but exports are more plausibly treated as exogenously determined.

The prediction of foreign capital requirements by the use of *ex-ante* 'saving' and 'trade' gap models requires *empirical* estimation of these parameters. This raises a number of problems about the meaning of these concepts, the degree of aggregation involved in their use and the difficulty of measuring their value from historical data for prediction. Each structural parameter will be examined in turn.

(i) *Marginal output–capital ratio*

The marginal or incremental output–capital ratio is used in most studies to predict the level of investment required to achieve a given growth in output for an economy. Some disaggregation is usually attempted since the economy's structure normally changes as it grows and different sectors have different coefficients. Instead of a single value of national product in any period, 'n' sectoral value-added magnitudes may be predetermined and each sector's required investment will be a function of value added in the sector. The aggregate of the sectoral investment requirements yields total investment requirements. It is usually easier to make a forecast of sectoral growth than aggregate growth and this procedure has the advantage that alternative estimates of investment needs can be made based on alternative development programmes or projected structures of an economy.

The problem still remains of obtaining a value for the marginal output–capital ratio for each sector which is basically defined as

$$\frac{\text{increase in value of output during year } t}{\text{investment in year } t.}$$

This may be in net or gross terms and it may involve a lag relating output changes to investment in any earlier period. This coefficient may be estimated from time series data. However, historical data usually show a very unstable relationship between investment and the increment of output. The reasons are obvious. Many factors other than investment in physical capital affect the addition to output or value added, particularly in the short period. The influence of technical change, availability of scarce manpower, degree of utilization of existing and additional capacity and (in the case of the agricultural sector especially) weather conditions, are all picked up and inputed to investment by the historical

98

approach to measurement of this relationship. It is not surprising that observed incremental output–capital ratios (aggregate and sectoral) are not statistically independent of growth rates but vary directly with them. (See H. Leibenstein, 'Incremental Capital–Output Ratios & Growth Rates in the Short Run', *Review of Economics & Statistics*, Vol. 48, February 1966.)

History does not always repeat itself; the coefficient derived from some past boom period and its particular technological conditions may not be a suitable guide to a future period when conditions may be completely different. Unfortunately, the estimation of foreign resource gaps over a short period of time (say 5 years) is particularly sensitive to the value of this parameter so that errors in its estimation can have very significant implications for foreign aid requirements.

(ii) *Marginal savings ratio*

The second major parameter of the growth models is the ratio of extra aggregate saving to extra aggregate income; the marginal savings ratio. When used for prediction there are problems arising from the high degree of aggregation involved in this concept. There are also difficulties in using historical data for estimating the value of the parameters, because shifts in the saving function can occur in developing economies if there is a growth in financial institutions and new opportunities for the use of savings as well as changes in government policies and tax/expenditure behaviour. It is useful to disaggregate into at least three major sectors – government, household and corporate and estimate savings functions for each sector.

In most developing countries *government savings* (i.e. excess of government current revenues over expenditures) play a very important role. The government savings function is particularly difficult to specify as it will depend on the existing tax structure, changes made in the tax structure and in tax rates, which depend on the political situation and attitude and strength of the country's rulers.

Since the majority of developing countries have a predominantly 'commodity' tax structure it may not be unreasonable to assume that government revenues would rise only proportionately with G.N.P. If government current expenditures rise in the same way, government savings would be proportional to G.N.P. However this limited elasticity of indirect tax systems in developing countries is not inevitable if changes in the tax structure are made.

Household savings behaviour in developing countries presents difficulties because of paucity of data. It is generally held that wage-earners have a very low or zero propensity to save in most developing countries. However, the household sector also includes peasants and owners of unincorporated enterprises who are considered by many economists to have high savings propensities out of disposable incomes. The savings behaviour of these groups may be strongly affected by institutional factors such as the extent of banking and credit insurance and pension institutions, savings propaganda and incentives, and the outcomes may well depend heavily on the institutional character of the economy and government policies with respect to savings.

Savings of the *corporate sector* should be isolated in developing countries because not only does it tend to have the highest sectoral propensity to save but it is usually the fastest growing sector in the economy.

In those semi-industrialized economies where the corporate sector largely serves the *domestic* market, some estimate of corporate savings may be made from the predetermined growth of value added in sectors like manufacturing, transport and public utilities where corporate organization is predominant. However, in many less developed countries, corporate organization can be identified with the *export sector* of the economy including the often foreign-owned mining, plantation and trading companies. In this case corporate profits and savings will be a function of the country's export earnings. Government saving may also be mainly affected by export earnings since much of their revenue often comes from indirect taxes on foreign trade and direct taxes on export companies. Savings will then tend to be a function of the largely *exogenous* factors which determine the future cycle and trend of exports of the particular commodities in which the economy specializes. Moreover, the marginal effect of profits and company savings will be larger, if the given change in export earnings is a result of a change in the price of exports rather than a change in their volume. More generally this influence of the terms of trade in an export economy can have a crucial effect on both savings behaviour and, of course, the value of exports when expressed in the *numeraire* of import prices.

(iii) *Marginal propensity to import*

Predicting the behaviour of imports is again likely to be more accurate if some disaggregation is attempted. To estimate the total import payments requires a distinction between debt service payments, invisible imports and visible imports. The main problem is to estimate visible imports. Two disaggregated approaches are possible; first by classifying imports by economic sector of destination and second by classifying imports by type of goods. The first procedure involves the use of an input–output matrix for the economy and is usually less practicable in most developing countries than one which classifies imports into (1) consumer goods (2) finished capital goods (3) raw materials and semi-finished (intermediate goods).

Imports of consumer goods are likely to be a fairly stable function of total national income. Imports of intermediate are usually a fairly stable function of value added in the manufacturing sector of the economy. The primary producing sector and the services sector of an economy are unlikely to be significant users of imported intermediate goods (with the exception of fertilizers and transport fuels). Capital goods import will be closely related to the sectoral investment levels since exports of capital goods are negligible in most developing countries.

The major conceptual problem in estimation of import requirements is to allow for the effect of *import-substitution* which occurs in a growing economy. It might be expected that investment in industries producing import substitutes would tend to reduce imports over time. In practice, although imports may fall as a proportion of G.N.P. they tend to *increase* absolutely with growth. The main explanation of this somewhat paradoxical result lies in some or all of the following factors.

a The establishment of new (import-saving) industries requires investment with a high import content. So long as the investment level and the (imported) capital–output ratio remains constant, the impact of this year's investment on the demand for imports should be more than offset by last year's investment in import substitutes now coming to fruition. However, if the investment level increases over time and the (imported) capital–output ratio rises with the move towards a more capital-intensive type of industry, then import requirements will not necessarily fall over time.

b Further, the additional output of these new industries increases the requirements of non-indigenous materials, fuels and components, etc. Hence the net import-substitution, or value added domestically, is often a small proportion of the value of the finished output.

c The additional income (wages and distributed profits) generated by the new activity creates extra expenditure on imported consumer goods and services. The effect on imported consumer goods will depend, among other things, on the government's domestic tax policies, the effective exchange rate and whether there are quantitative import controls.

This combination of forces can therefore result in rising import requirements over time, despite investment in import-saving industries. The precise outcome depends on so many parameters that no simple model can be constructed.

WITHDRAWN STATE UNIVERSITY COLLEGE FREDONIA, NEW YORK

Further reading

Three major works on economic aspects of aid are:
I. M. D. Little and J. Clifford, *International Aid*, 1965
R. Mikesell, *The Economics of Foreign Aid*, 1968.
L. B. Pearson (Chairman), *Partners in Development*, 1969.

Ch. 1. Politics and Statistics of Aid

The politics of aid has now developed a large literature. Some useful references are:
I. M. D. Little and J. Clifford, *International Aid*, chs. 1–3.
C. Kaplan, *The Challenge of Foreign Aid*, 1966.
Joan M. Nelson, *Aid, Influence & Foreign Policy*, 1968.
Tom Soper, 'Western Attitudes to Aid', *Lloyds Bank Review*, October 1969.

The main sources of statistics on assistance are the Development Assistance Committee of O.E.C.D., *Annual Review* and *The Flow of Financial Resources to Developing Countries* (Annual). United Nations; *International Flow of Long-Term Capital and Official Donations*, 1951–9 and Annual *World Economic Survey*. For the U.K., the Ministry of Overseas Development publishes annually *British Aid Statistics*. For official U.K. policy, reference should be made to the White Papers, Cmnd. 2147 and 2736 *Aid to Developing Countries*, 1963 and 1965. Cmnd. 3180 *Overseas Development: The Work in Hand*, 1967.

A further critical insight into the administration of the U.K. aid programme can be gained from a study of the Reports of the House of Commons Select Committee on Overseas Aid.

105

Ch. 2. Aid Sharing and Allocation

I. M. D. Little, *International Aid*, ch. 3.

J. Pincus, *Economic Aid & International Cost Sharing* (Rand), 1965, chs. 3 and 5.

'Cost of Foreign Aid', *Review of Economics & Statistics*, November 1963.

W. E. Schmidt, 'Economics of Charity', *Journal of Political Economy*, August 1964.

W. Kravis and J. Davenport 'The Political Arithmetic of International Burden Sharing', *Journal of Political Economy*, Vol. 71, No. 4, August 1963.

J. Fei and D. Paauw, 'Foreign Assistance & Self Help', *Review of Economics & Statistics*, Vol. 47, August 1965.

Ch. 3. Aid and Growth

R. McKinnon, 'Foreign Exchange Constraints in Economic Development', *Economic Journal*, June 1964. Reprinted in *International Trade*, Ed. J. Bhagwati (Penguin Modern Economics), 1968.

H. Chenery and A. Strout, 'Foreign Assistance & Economic Development', *American Economic Review*, Vol. 56, No. 4, September 1966.

Ch. 4. Estimating Aid Requirements

P. Rosenstein-Rodan, 'International Aid for Undeveloped Countries', *Review of Economics & Statistics*, Vol. 43, No. 2, May 1961.

G. Ohlin, *Foreign Aid Policies Reconsidered* (O.E.C.D.), 1966, ch. 4.

Chenery & Strout, *op. cit.*

J. Vanek, *Estimating Foreign Resource Needs for Economic Development*, New York, 1967, chs. 1 and 6 especially.

Ch. 5. Debt and Terms of Aid

D. Avramovic (Ed), *External Debt & Economic Growth* (I.B.R.D., Johns Hopkins) 1964, chs. 3 and 5.

G. M. Alter, 'The Servicing of Foreign Capital Inflows by Under-developed Countries' in *Economic Development for Latin America* (Eds. H. S. Ellis, H. C. Wallich) 1961.
Pearson, *op. cit.* ch. 8.

Ch. 6. Aid Tying

Little and Clifford, *op. cit.* ch. 7 and 12.
H. W. Singer, 'External Aid: For Plans or Projects', *Economic Journal*, September 1965.
A. Lovell, 'How Should Aid Be Given?', *Lloyds Bank Review*, April 1966.
J. Bhagwati, 'Tying of Aid', *UNCTAD. Doc. TD/7/Supp. 4*, 1 November 1967.
Empirical Estimates are given in 'The Cost of Tying to Recipient Countries', *UNCTAD Doc. TD/7/Supp. 8*, 21 November 1967.
Pearson, *op. cit.* ch. 9.

7 General Texts on Development Economics

H. Myint, *Economics of Developing Countries* (Oxford).
B. Higgins, *Economic Development* (Norton).
H. J. Bruton, *Development Economics*.

Ch. 8. Further Issues

L. Pearson, *Partners in Development*.
This covers the issues of performance criteria for aid and trade policies for development. This document, the product of an International Commission, is the latest and most comprehensive review of the development issue and it provides not only a good summary of the major policy issues in this field but also points the way forward to greater and more efficient international co-operation for aid and development.

HC
60
H383
1971b

*** SUNY Fredonia
3 0243 00061 311 7

TE DUE

RETURN
Nov 4
RETURNED
RETURN
May 13
May 13
RETU
May 13
URNED